The
BRISTOL AND GLOUCESTER RAILWAY

and the

AVON AND GLOUCESTERSHIRE RAILWAY

by
Colin G. Maggs

Gloucester passenger station 1846 – GWR porters transferring packages from one gauge to another. The dog is very unhappy with the situation.
Courtesy Illustrated London News

THE OAKWOOD PRESS

© Oakwood Press and Colin Maggs 1992

ISBN 0 85361 435 0

Typeset by Gem Publishing Company, Brightwell, Wallingford, Oxfordshire.

Printed by Alpha Print (Oxon) Ltd, Witney, Oxfordshire.

First Published 1969.

Second Enlarged Edition 1992.

The transhipment shed at Gloucester – narrow gauge wagon, *left*; broad gauge, *right*. The lad manning the crane handle appears to be in considerable danger.
Courtesy Illustrated London News

Published by
The OAKWOOD PRESS
P.O.Box 122, Headington, Oxford.

Contents

Acknowledgements

Acknowledgements for assistance are due to W. Bagnall; J. Barber; B. Edwards; Sir Arthur Elton; J. Ferris; J. Gardner; G. Hemmings; T. King; R.S. Howlett; D. Payne; G. Pothecary; E.W. Plowright; W. Powell; M.J.H. Southway; D. Thorne; C.H.A. Townley; A. Woolrich and K. White.

Note: The abbreviation 'B&GR' applies to the Bristol & Gloucester Railway; the Bristol and Gloucester*shire* Railway is always set out in full.

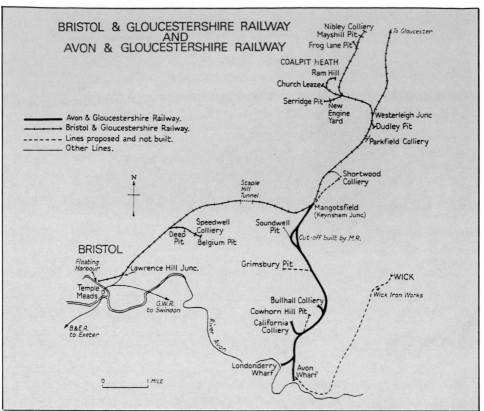

BRISTOL & GLOUCESTERSHIRE RAILWAY
AND
AVON & GLOUCESTERSHIRE RAILWAY

Avon & Gloucestershire Railway.
Bristol & Gloucestershire Railway.
Lines proposed and not built.
Other Lines.

Nibley Colliery
Mayshill Pit
Frog Lane Pit
To Gloucester
COALPIT HEATH
Ram Hill
Church Leaze
Serridge Pit
New Engine Yard
Westerleigh Junc
Dudley Pit
Parkfield Colliery

N

Staple Hill Tunnel

Shortwood Colliery

Mangotsfield
(Keynsham Junc.)

Speedwell Colliery
Soundwell Pit
Deep Pit
Belgium Pit
Cut-off built by M.R.

BRISTOL
Floating Harbour
Lawrence Hill Junc.
Grimsbury Pit
WICK
Wick Iron Works
Temple Meads
G.W.R. to Swindon
Bullhall Colliery
Cowhorn Hill Pit
California Colliery
B&E.R. to Exeter
River Avon
Londonderry Wharf
Avon Wharf

0   1 MILE

In June 1947, awaiting the signals to Barnwood shed, Gloucester is LMS No. 1097 (of 22B Gloucester shed) at Eastgate station, with the Great Western Horton Road shed in the background.

Roger Venning

Chapter One

The Bristol & Gloucestershire Railway

In the latter half of the 18th century, Bristol was a flourishing city and required coal for its developing glass, pottery, sugar refining, brewing, distilling, soap making and smelting industries. There were some pits close to the city, and more coal was readily available at Coalpit Heath, 9 miles to the north; but road transport by packhorse or wagon was difficult and expensive. Often in the winter, mines were only worked two or three days a week because of the difficulty of transporting the coal.

In February 1783, Lord Middleton, one of the Coalpit Heath colliery proprietors, wrote to his partner Thomas Smyth of Stapleton, proposing a canal straight out of the colliery levels to Bristol, to save the expense of horse gins raising coal and also to ease the surface transport. Nothing was done, and, nearly three years later, in January 1786 he wrote: 'Can a wood wagon way be got to Bristol from ye Colliery, or can one be got to ye Canal yt is cutting from ye Severn to ye Thames?' In 1788, 1792 and 1793 further canal schemes were proposed, but proved abortive.

In 1803 a railway was proposed from Coalpit Heath to the harbour at Bristol at a cost of £23,000. The money could not be raised and the scheme died. The following year there was a proposal for a wagonway from Coalpit Heath to the Avon near Bitton, with a branch running to Hanham Mills. In 1812 and 1814, plans for a line to Bristol itself were put forward, but came to naught. Then on 13th December, 1824, a well-supported meeting was held in the White Lion Inn, Bristol, presided over by the mayor, Thomas Hassell, with the object of building a single line to Birmingham via Gloucester, Tewkesbury and Worcester. The meeting was supposed to have been a private one held at the office of Osborne & Ward, the company's solicitors, but the attendance was so great that they adjourned to the White Lion.

The Bristol, Northern & Western Railway as it was known, would have provided a useful link between the manufacturing area of Birmingham and the sea, and also given a rail outlet to the collieries at Coalpit Heath. The £50 shares were allotted as follows: 16,000 to Bristol, 1,000 to Gloucester, 1,500 to Worcester, 2,500 to Birmingham, 1,000 to Ireland and 3,000 to land-owners. The total was £1,250,000.

When the subscription list was opened at the meeting, 'a complete scramble took place, in which much ink was upset and pens spoilt in the eagerness of all to subscribe, and before the meeting broke up the whole number of shares allotted to Bristol were taken'; £350,000 was raised in one hour. Each of these shares required a deposit of 40 shillings within 48 hours.

On 28th January, 1825, the Bristol, Northern & Western Railway appointed Josias Jessop, resident engineer and Robert Fletcher, accountant. Apart from the railway carrying goods to and from Birmingham, it was expected to capture the brick and clay traffic of Stourbridge, the salt of Droitwich, the products from the woollen mills of the Stroud valley and coal and paving stone from Coalpit Heath.

Members of the provisional committee of the Bristol, Northern & Western Railway elected 13th December, 1824, were:

Thomas Hassell	(George Lunnell)
William Edward Acraman	Richard Nott
Henry Browne	(James Ezekial Nash)*
Robert Bush*	Charles Payne*
Robert Bright*	Thomas Reynolds
Lieut.-General Browne	George Eddie Sanders
Henry Bush*	Robert Suple
Edward Rolle Clayfield	John Nash Sanders
Michael Hinton Castle	Thomas Stock*
(Daniel Fripp)*	Sir Richard Vaughan
(Christopher George)*	(Matthew Wright)
George Gibbs	(Henry Overton Wills)
Thomas Kington*	

Names in brackets were not on the permanent committee, and persons marked * were proprietors of the Bristol & Gloucestershire Railway.

The permanent committee was appointed on 21st January, 1825 and the name of Thomas Fussell, an ironmaster of Mells, was added to the above list.

By June 1825, W.H. Townsend, a local surveyor and valuer, who was later to survey the Bristol end of the GWR and was one of the three unsuccessful candidates competing with I.K. Brunel for the post of Engineer to that railway, had surveyed the line almost to Worcester, but found that a line from Worcester to Birmingham would be difficult, as inclined planes and heavy cuttings and embankments could not be avoided, because of the topography. A Bristol terminus was planned at Stokes Croft, with a branch to the Floating Harbour. An inclined plane would have taken the railway out of the Frome valley near Bristol and another inclined plane was to have been built at Falfield. On 15th June, 1825, the committee agreed that the line from Bristol to Worcester should be built, but the rest of the line to Birmingham deferred. Unfortunately, landowners objected to the proposed route out of Bristol, and because of the topography, an alternative was difficult to find. In October the Committee announced that parliamentary powers would not be sought that session and £20,000 was to be invested in Exchequer Bills.

In March 1826, Jessop estimated the cost of the line to Worcester at £362,221; to Gloucester at £224,383 or to the Gloucester & Berkeley Canal at only £160,790. However the financial crisis of 1826 caused a large number of subscribers to call for a complete abandonment of the project and a return of the deposit money, and this course was agreed to at a special meeting on 19th May, 1826. It was remarkable that 17s. 6d. in the pound was returned to subscribers, only 2s. 6d. being kept to cover administrative costs and legal expenses.

The need for a railway did not diminish, as the annual coal consumption at Bristol in 1827 was 240,000 tons. On 27th October, 1827 several gentlemen connected with Bristol resolved to build a double line from Bristol to Coalpit Heath. The provisional committee of this the Bristol & Gloucestershire Railway consisted of Alderman George, Sheriff Payne, Dr John New, Henry Bush, George Jones, John Evans Lunnell, John Winwood,

John Hare, junior and Richard Ricketts. The cost of a double line was estimated to be £49,727 and a single line about £9,000 cheaper; £16,000 was subscribed by Christmas Eve. The Kennet & Avon Canal Company suggested a branch should run to the Avon near Keynsham and this proposal was adopted.

The Bristol & Gloucestershire, or Coalpit Heath railway as it was often called, was surveyed and engineered by W.H. Townsend, assisted by Urquhart, resident surveyor. The line ran from Cuckold's Pill, later Avon Street depot, Bristol Harbour, to Orchard Pit at Coalpit Heath. Townsend made what he thought was an accurate estimate of the single line, £41,819 14s. 2d., though in the event, its actual cost was almost £9,000 per mile, making the total cost for the 9 miles £83,636 4s. 2d.

The Act 9 Geo.IV cap. 93 received the Royal Assent on 19th June, 1828. It allowed the Bristol & Gloucestershire to build a line to carry coal and stone from pits and quarries at Coalpit Heath and also to carry other goods. The capital was £45,000 in £50 shares, with borrowing powers of £12,000. Four-fifths of the capital had already been subscribed, but all had to be raised before the railway could be built. A minimum of £40 out of every £100 had to be spent on the line north of Rodway Hill, Mangotsfield, as this northern section was to be used by the Avon & Gloucestershire Railway (A&GR), a line largely promoted by the Kennet & Avon Canal (see later). Five years were allowed for completion; 12 months elapsed before the subscribers had met the amount of the estimate. At first it was intended to build only a single line, but after the undertaking had commenced it was thought best to build earthworks for double line (though in fact only a single line was laid), and this extra work delayed the opening. Tenders for earthwork and masonry for the northern section were advertised for in January 1829 and for laying blocks and rails and 'sreining the upper portion of the said railway' in August 1830.

The northern half of the line (from Mangotsfield to Coalpit Heath) was opened in July 1832 for use by the Avon & Gloucestershire Railway, but the southern section was delayed. The borrowing powers of £12,000 had been used up and the line was still not completed. An Act, 4–5 Will. IV cap. 102 of 26th March, 1834, allowed the company to raise a further £20,000 either in £50 shares, or by borrowing and also granted a three-years extension of time for completion. On 27th December, 1834, 282 ft of Staple Hill tunnel were completed from the west mouth; 97 ft at the first shaft; 131 ft from the second shaft; and 240 ft from the east mouth. The opening of the Bristol & Gloucestershire Railway took place on 6th August, 1835. The first wagon of the opening procession held a band and it was followed by seven more wagons, which had been converted at Bristol to carry shareholders and friends to Coalpit Heath. The committee were in a wagon specially fitted by Richard Stratton, a Bristol wheelwright, timber dealer and wrought iron manufacturer. Ladies were carried in two closed cars with green baize seats for 14 passengers. Each wagon was drawn by a horse. The first wagon in the procession left St Philip's, Bristol, at 10.30 am. The embankments, cuttings and bridges were crowded with spectators for the opening of Bristol's first railway. Passengers were no doubt relieved that the two shafts of the

515 yds-long Staple Hill tunnel had been left open to give light. At the eastern portal of the tunnel the procession was met by two carriages from Westerleigh and together with another band, they proceeded to Coalpit Heath. The procession arrived there at 1.30 pm, having covered the 9 miles in three hours, and the hundred guests walked to a tent for luncheon. The company Chairman, George Jones, in his speech, said that coal at Bristol would be 5s. to 6s. a ton cheaper (hitherto the price had been 16s. to 20s. a ton). The 340 workmen and colliers dined outside the tent on tables set in a field. At 5 pm the party left with 50 wagons carrying 200 tons of 'extra ordinary fine coal'. Nearly all this coal was bought by J.A. Smart, a St Philip's coal merchant. The procession extended for almost a mile.

'The most interesting part of the journey,' wrote The Bristol Gazette, 'was the descent of the inclined plane* where the horses were removed and carriages impelled forward by force of gravitation. For some distance they proceeded at the rate of a quick trot, but so great was the command by which the guides (brakesmen) were possessed, by means of a lever acting upon the wheels, that though even here several stoppages took place, there was not the least danger of a collision.' The train finally arrived at St Philip's about 8.30 that evening.

It was fortunate that the lie of the land favoured loaded trains. There was a rise of 1 in 528 from Coalpit Heath to Shortwood followed by a level section to the southern end of Staple Hill tunnel, and then a fall of 1 in 71 to the River Avon, about 175 ft below the level of the tunnel.

Bristol now turned to communications with London. W.H. Townsend was one of the surveyors whose names were put forward to the Great Western Railway Bristol committee for building a cheap line to London, but I.K. Brunel was eventually chosen. Brunel first suggested using the Bristol & Gloucestershire line, and then going across country from Wick to Lambridge on the eastern outskirts of Bath, but then he settled on the present route using the Avon valley.

As detailed in the next chapter, the Bristol & Gloucestershire Railway now became involved in the larger ambitions of the Bristol & Gloucester Railway. The conversion of the line from Bristol to Westerleigh to main line standard (broad gauge) started in 1843 and was left as late as possible so that traffic would be held up for a minimum period. As it happened, coal traffic had not been so heavy that year as a result of the economic depression; in August 1843, the Directors said that the line was being improved without hindering traffic. The Bristol & Gloucester Railway paid the Bristol & Gloucestershire £239 13s. 6d. for loss of traffic during the conversion from standard to broad gauge. The dividend for the year 1843–44 was 5 per cent, with a final dividend of £1 7s. 6d. per share in September 1844. With the opening of the Bristol & Gloucester Railway on 8th July, 1844, the Bristol & Gloucestershire merged with it as authorised by Act 2–3 Vic. cap. 56 of 1st July, 1839.

Permanent Way

The gauge was 4 ft 8 in. and the maximum distance to the outside edges 5 ft 1 in. The malleable cast iron rails weighed 35 lb./yd. and were 15 ft long, of fish-bellied type with five webs. The rails were held to stone blocks by

---

* The 1 in 55 incline between Lawrence Hill Junction and Fishponds.

iron chairs and rail joints were supported in one chair. In places, wooden sleepers were laid on stone blocks and chairs attached to the sleepers. Owners of adjoining land were allowed to make 'Openings in the Ledges or Flanches . . . as may be necessary . . . for effecting a Communication with the Railway'.

At first the Bristol & Gloucestershire Railway paid 1s. 4d. for each stone block, but then bought them from the Avon & Gloucestershire's quarry at 1s. for a 16 in. square block of 10 in. depth, and 1s. 8d. for a 20 in. block, delivered at Rodway Hill Junction.

Rates and Regulations

At a meeting on 16th July, 1835, the rates and tolls were discussed, and whether to provide locomotives, but unfortunately no details of this meeting are now known. The Act stated that tolls should not exceed 2d. to 4d. per ton/mile for various stipulated commodities, and the charge for coal, culm or coke going to the Avon & Gloucestershire Railway was not to exceed 5d. per ton/mile. After having their wagons run on a weighbridge, the carriers were given tickets specifying the weight carried. Passengers in their own coaches were to be charged 2½d. per mile; large animals such as horses and cows charged 1½d. each and smaller ones such as sheep, ¼d. a mile.

The company had to set up ¼-mile posts and at every toll gate had a Table of Tolls, with black letters on a white ground giving the name of the gate, and a list of rates. The name of the toll collector was written either on the board or on the toll house. The Act allowed the rates to be farmed out, except to proprietors of collieries within 5 miles of the line.

The rules stated: 'No locomotive engine shall be used for propelling, but only drawing power, except for taking turnouts'. Every driver (of a horse) or engineman 'neglecting to blow his horn 150 yards before passing any public road . . . shall forfeit Forty Shillings'. A fine of 20 shillings was imposed if the points were not re-set for the main line. If two loaded, or unloaded, trains met, the one for Bristol took the turnout, or if they met between turnouts, the train going up had to put back into the nearest turnout. Every unloaded train meeting a loaded one took the turnout, and if it was between turnouts, had to set back to allow the loaded one to proceed without delay.

Every train not moved by steam had to give way to steam, except between the company's Bristol Yard and the 3 mile post, 'in which case the steam train will set back to enable the loaded carriages to pass through the nearest turnout. Every non-steam train on being overtaken by steam, to put into the nearest turnout.'

The Bristol & Gloucestershire company's seal had the Bristol coat of arms dexter and the Gloucestershire arms sinister.

Locomotives

In 1829 the Bristol press suggested that one of Sir Goldsworthy Gurney's steam carriages should be tried out on the line. The previous year one had been tried on the road between London and Bath and others were in service at Cheltenham later.

There were three Coalpit Heath colliery proprietors: Sir John Smyth who held half the capital and Lord Middleton and E.F. Colston who held a quarter each. A letter in the Ashton Court Collection* written by Sir John Smyth to E.F. Colston on 2nd February, 1835 said 'The Bristol & Gloucestershire Railway is now approaching completion' and 'the railway Company have determined on providing the Locomotive Power.' Another letter on 23rd February gave the toll as '4½d. per ton for Locomotive Power, 4d. per ton Waggons'. Later this letter explained that Bond & Windwood's steam carriage had exploded, sending parts 300 yds away after a modification had been made to increase its speed in order that it could make two, instead of one trip daily. It had its steam 'generated in tubes, not in the boiler, to render it more safe'. It was a small locomotive, and the colliery proprietors were trying to make it do until 'we can get some proper sized steam carriages on the Rail Road similar to those in use at the Welsh Collieries, Iron Works and elsewhere'.

Even before the explosion, Colston was so keen on using locomotives that he had given a definite order to Acraman's, Bristol engineers, to build a locomotive, whereas Lord Middleton, only intended that Colston should sound out Acraman on the possibility of ordering one. No more is known of locomotive power on the line.

Wagons

The rolling stock had to conform with the orders and regulations. The name of the owner, the wagon's number and weight had to be painted in white letters at least 2 inches high on the sides of the wagons and coaches. 'Every wagon to be constructed to dimensions and according to the drawing deposited in the company's yard, Bristol.' The Act limited four-wheeled wagons to a load of 4 tons, or as the bye-laws of 16th July, 1835 put it, 5 tons including the weight of the wagon, or a six-wheeled wagon, 6 tons. The wagon owners were responsible for damage done by their rolling stock, and the wagons or carriages were not permitted 'without the License of the company . . . to pass upon the Railway or Tramroad', at any other times than between the hours of 7 am to 6 pm (November–February), 6 am–8 pm (March–April and September–October), and 5 am–10 pm (May–August) – chiefly the daylight hours.

At the St Philip's coal shed, a horse-worked windlass drew wagons up an incline and the coal was discharged into bunkers under the track.

* Held in the Bristol Record Office.

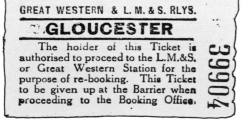

Chapter Two

The Bristol & Gloucester Railway

The Bristol & Gloucestershire Railway had been successful up to a point, but an extension to Gloucester was needed. An original survey had been made in 1833 by I.K. Brunel and was supplementary to the Birmingham & Gloucester survey made when he was employed by the brothers Joseph and Charles Sturge of Birmingham. He made a second survey in 1838 and reduced earthworks and curves within the parliamentary limits of deviation.

On 4th November, 1835 a prospectus was issued stating that the Bristol & Gloucestershire had been originally laid down under the advice of Jessop, with the express view of future extension northward and was constructed to permit doubling. The Birmingham & Gloucester line was sanctioned in 1836, but the Bristol & Gloucestershire extension was refused in February 1838, mainly due to opposition in Gloucester. After the GWR assented to the plan and backed it up with £50,000, the scheme was again presented to Parliament.

The Bill was read for the first time on 7th March, 1839, the second time on 19th March and the third time on 13th May when it was passed. The Act (2–3 Vic. cap. 56) received the Royal Assent on 1st July, 1839. It allowed the Bristol & Gloucester Railway (B&GR) to absorb the Bristol & Gloucestershire and to extend the line from Westerleigh, 2 miles short of Coalpit Heath, to Standish Junction, a distance of 21½ miles; from Standish they were to negotiate with the Cheltenham & Great Western Union Railway (C&GWUR), then under construction, to lay a third rail to Gloucester and the Bristol & Gloucestershire's original gauge of 4ft 8in. was repealed, except for the section used by the A&GR. The Act allowed the Bristol & Gloucester to raise a capital of £400,000 with borrowing powers of £133,000.

The first meeting of the Bristol & Gloucester Company took place at Bristol on 11th July, 1839, when George Jones and nine others met in Robert Fletcher's offices in the Exchange Buildings, Bristol. George Jones was elected Chairman and Robert Fletcher Secretary. Brunel urged an immediate commencement of the survey and recommended George Hennett for the job. Hennett started in mid-July and completed his survey in 16 weeks. On 31st August, 1839 a Committee of Management of 15 members was appointed and £1,000 allotted to be divided between them annually. The committee was composed of:

Joseph Frankel Alexander	Francis Fry
Henry Bush	Henry Fyson
Samuel Baker	George Jones
Frederick Ricketts	William Morgan
Thomas Rankin	William Ford Mogg
Silas Dibsdall	John Winwood
Alexander Wright Daniel	James Maurice Shipton
	Richard Ricketts

On 9th September, I.K. Brunel was invited to be Engineer. In a letter inviting him, George Jones wrote saying that the Coalpit Heath line from Bristol to the proposed junction at Westerleigh would not be disturbed. 'It is proposed that narrow gauge be adopted – this, of course, follows in

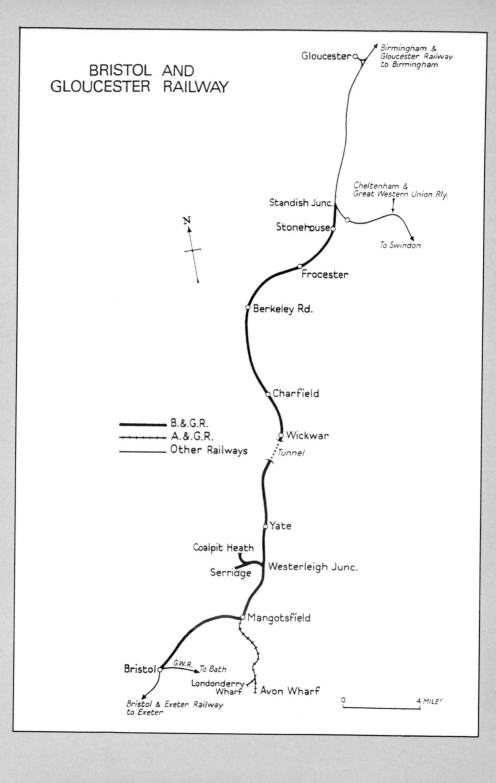

BRISTOL AND
GLOUCESTER RAILWAY

Gloucester

Birmingham &
Gloucester Railway
to Birmingham

Cheltenham &
Great Western Union Rly.

Standish Junc.

Stonehouse

To Swindon

N

Frocester

Berkeley Rd.

Charfield

Wickwar

Tunnel

B. & G.R.
A. & G.R.
Other Railways

Yate

Coalpit Heath

Westerleigh Junc.

Serridge

Mangotsfield

Bristol

G.W.R. To Bath

Londonderry
Wharf

Avon Wharf

Bristol & Exeter Railway
to Exeter

0   4 MILES

accordance with the foregoing.' Also 'that continuous longitudinal bearing be *not* adopted and that the Extension line be constructed at an outlay not exceeding the means at their disposal.'

Brunel accepted the offer on 12th September and said that he had no objection to narrow gauge in the existing circumstances. J.W. Hammond was appointed Resident Engineer from 1st February, 1841, and Harrison, Assistant Engineer, from the same date; both came from the GWR.

On 2nd January, 1840 a letter was received from the Deputy Chairman of the Birmingham & Gloucester Railway proposing a union of the two lines. A special meeting of the Bristol & Gloucester was held next day and a deputation from both railways met at Gloucester on 6th January. A deputation from the C&GWUR was invited to join the joint deputations the following day and take over the joint railways. The Cheltenham Directors met them, but declined the offer; the C&GWUR was in serious financial difficulties through arrears of calls on shares.

At a meeting on 11th January, the Bristol and Birmingham companies agreed that a union was of mutual benefit, and proposed they should purchase the C&GWUR, half the purchase to be in cash and half in stock of the united companies. With union in sight, Birmingham looked closely at the Bristol line and found it was 'ill-chosen, both as respects its costs, gradients and traffic to be expected on it'. Birmingham proposed a new and cheaper line to Bristol following the coast and passing the pier at Aust Ferry and the proposed dock project at Shirehampton, the line terminating at Cumberland Basin, Bristol. Comparative costs were:

Wickwar Line	£
Making Coalpit Heath line double	55,500
New line to Gloucester	629,570
Plus other items making total	£906,860
Aust Line	£
Works	391,225
Plus other items making total	£646,038

Income from the Wickwar line was estimated at £43,042 – 4¾ per cent of outlay, and the income from the Aust line £60,080 – 9⅓ per cent. Tunnelling on the Aust line would have been less than half that on the Wickwar line. However, in March 1840, the Bristol company decided to drop amalgamation, as it could not agree with the Birmingham Board on the modified proposal to be made to the C&GWUR.

At the general meeting on 31st March, 1840 it was reiterated that narrow gauge was adopted, as most of the traffic would be from Birmingham and the north to Bristol, and that they were negotiating with the C&GWUR to lay additional rails between Standish and Gloucester. At a meeting with the C&GWUR on 17th November, 1840 it was agreed that the third rail would be laid and maintained between Standish and Gloucester at B&GR expense and

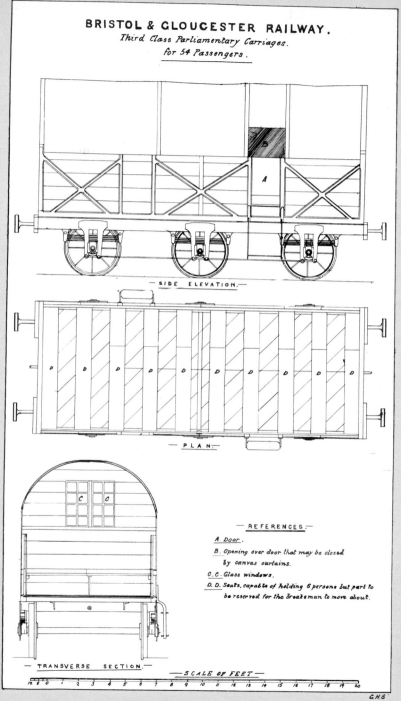

BRISTOL & GLOUCESTER RAILWAY.

Third Class Parliamentary Carriages.
for 54 Passengers.

— SIDE ELEVATION. —

— PLAN. —

— TRANSVERSE SECTION. —

— REFERENCES. —

A. *Door.*

B. *Opening over door that may be closed by canvas curtains.*

C.C. *Glass windows.*

D.D. *Seats, capable of holding 6 persons but part to be reserved for the brakesman to move about.*

— SCALE OF FEET —

12 6 0 1 2 3 4 5 6 7 8 9 10 11 12 13 14 15 16 17 18 19 20

C.H.S

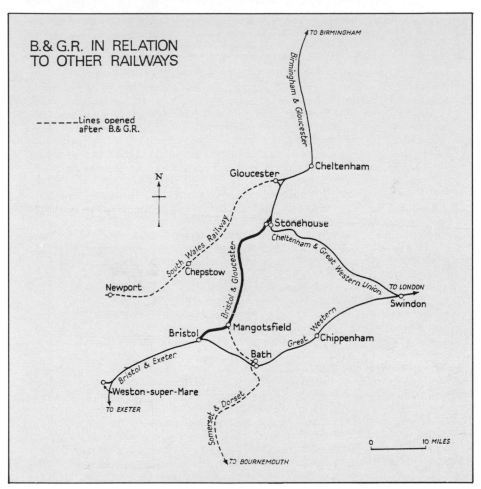

B.& G.R. IN RELATION
TO OTHER RAILWAYS

------- Lines opened
after B.& G.R.

N

TO BIRMINGHAM

Birmingham & Gloucester

Cheltenham

Gloucester

South Wales Railway

Chepstow

Newport

Stonehouse

Cheltenham & Great Western Union

TO LONDON

Swindon

Bristol & Gloucester

Bristol

Mangotsfield

Bath

Great Western

Chippenham

Bristol & Exeter

Weston-super-Mare

TO EXETER

Somerset & Dorset

TO BOURNEMOUTH

0   10 *MILES*

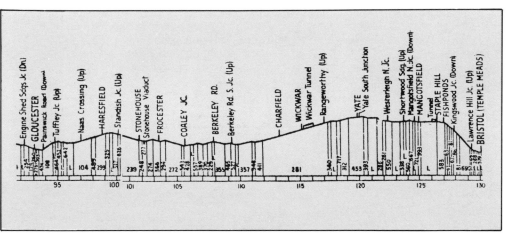

15

remain B&GR property. The B&GR asked for a firm date for the completion of the Standish to Gloucester line, but the C&GWUR was vague, and merely committed itself to say that it would be the last section to be finished.

Although the B&GR had seemingly settled for narrow gauge, a special report was now called for to consider adopting broad gauge. Brunel calculated that an extra foot width from Bristol to Standish would only cost an extra £6,968, and suggested that if the line was to be made broad gauge at a later date, only the masonry of tunnels, bridges and embankments need now be wider, as the rock sides of the tunnel could be widened and in cuttings the open ditches could be replaced by tile drains giving more space.

Work started on the B&GR in 1841, all the heaviest work being in hand by April. In September, a proposal was submitted to the Cheltenham & Great Western Union Railway for parliamentary powers being obtained for the B&GR to build the Standish Junction to Gloucester line, the C&GWUR paying half the costs. Parliamentary sanction for this was given in the C&GWUR Act, 5–6 Vic. cap. 28, 13th May, 1842. On 28th October, 1842, notice was given to the C&GWUR that the B&GR Directors intended to appoint a committee conforming with the provision of this Act, so that, subject to powers of re-purchase by the C&GWUR, the B&GR could build the line from Standish to Gloucester, the section to be governed by a committee of five from each company – though in the event, the GWR purchased the C&GWUR and completed the line itself.

In his report on 30th March, 1842, Brunel stated that all the contracts were let. The company had adopted the policy of using small contractors, so that risk was lessened and this allowed more contractors to compete, leading to lower tenders. The B&GR Act, 5–6 Vic. cap. 46 of 18th June, 1842 gave an extension of time for two years for purchasing land and allowed a further capital of £200,000 shares and borrowing powers of £66,000.

On 13th December, 1842, the B&GR sub-committee was told by Charles Russell, Chairman of the GWR, the rental his company would charge the B&GR for using the line from Standish to Gloucester. On traffic receipts up to £23,000 a rental of £12,000 was required and 50 per cent on further traffic. On the line between Gloucester and Cheltenham the rental was £5,000 on receipts up to £9,000 and 60 per cent on traffic beyond £9,000. The rent of Gloucester station would be £1,000 and Cheltenham station another £1,000. Russell also said that the Great Western would be prepared to work the line from Bristol to Standish for:

    60% on the first £50,000 of traffic receipts
    55% on the next £25,000 of traffic receipts
    50% on the next £25,000 of traffic receipts
    45% on the next £25,000 of traffic receipts
    40% on the next £25,000 of traffic receipts
    Maintenance charges to be paid by the B&GR

The B&GR thought these terms too high and offered £12,000 for the Standish to Cheltenham line for traffic up to £22,000; 50 per cent on traffic £22,000 to £25,000 and 45 per cent on traffic beyond. For the use of the stations at Gloucester and Cheltenham it offered £1,250. Terms for the Bristol to Standish line it suggested as being:

50% on all traffic up to £50,000
40% on all traffic up to £75,000
35% on all traffic beyond

The Great Western deputation declined these terms as they amounted to less than it cost them to work their own lines, and the B&GR came to the conclusion it would be able to work trains more cheaply itself.

An important change in policy was announced at the general meeting 29th March, 1843. It was stated that the GWR was taking over the C&GWUR (the transfer formally took place on 1st July, 1843), and had leased the Bristol & Exeter Railway since the proposal to build the B&GR had been made. Passengers needed through coaches, or at the very least, wanted to be able to change trains easily without leaving the station. Brunel therefore urged a change to the broad gauge, though the Chairman, George Jones, opposed the measure. An arrangement with the Birmingham & Gloucester would have been admirable for traffic from the north to Bristol, but for passengers travelling beyond, the separate stations at Bristol would have seriously inconvenienced passengers. Also, a narrow gauge B&GR would have been in competition with the Great Western, who would no doubt have retaliated by routeing passengers and goods from Gloucester to Bristol via Swindon.

An arrangement was made with the GWR on 13th April, 1843 (it was signed, but not sealed, and in 1858 this led to a dispute when the Midland Railway repudiated the agreement on the ground that it was not sealed), which saved the B&GR an outlay of £40,000 to £50,000 and annual economies by the joint use of the Great Western's passenger and goods stations at Bristol, Gloucester and Cheltenham; the only extra expense was a ½-mile line from the B&GR from Lawrence Hill to the GWR at Temple Meads, Bristol. Powers for building this spur were given in 6–7 Vic cap. 54, 27th June, 1843.

The B&GR was to have running powers over GWR lines for 20 years, at charges of £11,000 per annum (Standish to Gloucester), and £4,000 per annum (Gloucester to Cheltenham). (In December 1843, it decided not to use these latter running powers.) The B&GR could use the GWR stations at Bristol, Gloucester and Cheltenham for £3,500 and enjoy 'the requisite accommodation for carriages and passengers, booking clerks, police and other assistants to attend to passengers and their luggage' and also 'the necessary accommodation at the goods shed for merchandise traffic exclusive of minerals'. After the first five years, the total payments were to be increased by £1,000 a year together with a proportion of any revenue exceeding £30,000. The GWR promised to complete the double line from Standish to Gloucester by April 1844.

At Gloucester the break of gauge was not expected to be inconvenient, as passengers from Birmingham could simply step across the platform from one train to another. The B&GR therefore had to become a broad gauge line; but the only additional cost would be less than £5,000 for the extra ballast, and at the same time saving the £30,000 cost of laying a third rail between

Standish and Gloucester. As works were in quite an advanced state, the line was never full broad gauge width, Wickwar and Staple Hill tunnels being only 26 ft wide, and underbridges the same between the parapets. Clearances were small, as Great Western broad gauge coaches measured 11 ft 5 in. over the lower footboards, which would have only left about 10 in. between the footboard and tunnel wall and 18 in. between footboards of passing coaches.

By the terms of the agreement, the B&GR undertook:

(a)   to make its line broad gauge;
(b)   to establish a physical connection between the B&GR and the GWR at Bristol;
(c)   to subscribe £50,000 to the cost of the South Devon Railway which was pushing the broad gauge to Plymouth.

The *Railway Times* commented that the B&GR had 'bound themselves hand and foot, henceforth and for ever' to the GWR, though in the event, this was far from the truth. An indirect advantage of the adoption of broad gauge was that Coalpit Heath coal could be taken to the industrial Stroud valley, whereas competition would not have allowed the expense of a gauge transfer.

In 1843 Brunel said that there was insufficient work for Hammond to spend all his time on the line, so his salary was reduced to £300 from 25th March, and Harrison and Brereton were removed altogether. At the half yearly meeting it was announced that alterations to the existing Coalpit

Class '4F' 0−6−0 No. 44272 halts at Berkeley Road with the 1.10 pm (Saturdays-only) Bristol−Gloucester stopping train, 14th June, 1958.   *R.E. Toop*

Heath line had already started. George Jones, Francis Fry and Christopher Shapland made another visit north in the summer of 1843, to find the most economical way of working the line, as the Great Western terms of 45 per cent on traffic receipts were thought too expensive. On 29th September, 1843, Stothert, Slaughter & Company's tender for working seven trains each way for £18,500 a year was accepted. As well as providing locomotives and rolling stock, Stothert, Slaughter & Co., were to look after the line entirely, and the B&GR avoided an outlay for repair shops, carriage sheds, engine houses and coke ovens. In May 1844, Stothert, Slaughter asked the B&GR to seek permission from the GWR to erect and paint the carriages in Bristol station and also to give the locomotives trial runs on the GWR. In August 1843, Brunel was able to report that a third of the widening of Staple Hill tunnel was complete, 4 miles of permanent way had been laid and track was in the process of being laid on the spur between Lawrence Hill and the GWR station at Bristol.

In November the Bristol Infirmary made a special application to the B&GR as 13 'expensive casualties' had been sent from the line during the course of the previous 12 months. The B&GR added £20 to its usual subscription of five guineas.

In November tenders for building stations were accepted:

Station	£	s.	Contractor
Charfield	1,420	0	George Hawkins
Berkeley	1,843	0	George Hawkins
Yate	1,648	0	Benjamin Farmer
Frocester	1,524	18	Benjamin Farmer
Wickwar	220	0	John Gay
	£6,655	18	

George Hawkins went bankrupt and his work was finished by Samuel Bromhead, one of his sureties. Benjamin Farmer also erected a passenger and goods station at Stonehouse and coaltips at Wickwar, Charfield, Berkeley Road, Frocester and Stonehouse.

Before contractors began any excavations, or formed embankments, all the top soil or turf had to be removed and if the soil under the embankment was wet, it had to be excavated to a depth of 18 in. The finished line was fenced with split oak posts, 7 ft long which had a minimum cross section of 14 sq. in. The posts were set 9 ft apart and 4 ft above the surface of the ground and morticed to receive the end of the four horizontal oak or larch rails. The whole was stiffened by an intermediate small upright post of oak or larch.

A ditch was formed within the fence and material was excavated to form a quick mound between the ditch and the slope. Draining tiles were laid through the quick mound at intervals of not more than 20 yds. The earthworks were carefully finished. 'The faces of slopes are to be neatly covered with turfs of grass not less than 8 in. thickness with green sward outwards and well beat and pressed into place.' If the turf which had been kept was not considered good enough by the engineer, 8 in. of topsoil had to be sown with ryegrass and clover seed mixed, not less than 14 lb. of clover seed and 1 bushel of ryegrass per acre. Before putting filling between the wingwalls and abutments of bridges, red marl had to be broken into small lumps and carefully packed to prevent settling. George Hall was paid 8d. per cu. yd. for his contract; nine-tenths was paid, but the remaining tenth withheld until the completion of a year's maintenance.

Careful attention was paid to the appearance of the line, £60 being paid to John Nelson for planting shrubs and forest trees at five of the company's stations. The stations were lit by naphtha lamps, but as the light they gave was insufficient, Firman's contract was closed in December 1844 and they were replaced by oil lamps.

Wyndham Harding, general superintendent of the line, started work on 14th June, 1844; his previous post had been general superintendent and Secretary of the Glasgow & Greenock Railway. He had been a contemporary at Rugby School of Thomas Hughes, author of *Tom Brown's Schooldays*. It was highly unusual for a classical scholar to take up engineering. Harding became a pupil under Thomas Gooch, brother of Daniel. Eventually Harding became Secretary of the LSWR where John Gooch, yet another brother, was locomotive superintendent.

The bye-laws were adopted on 18th June. One read that if there was not room in the train at an intermediate station, those booked for the longest journey should have preference. 'Smoking is strictly prohibited both in and upon the Carriages and in the Company's stations.'

The financial statement up to 30th June stated that receipts totalled £610,436 4s. 10d., with expenses of £501,177 16s. 6d. including Parliamentary cost of £25,589 7s. 10d.

Wickwar station view looking south c.1905. The station master stands on the down platform observing the photographer; two milk churns are placed at its far end.

M.J. Tozer Collection

Chapter Three
The Bristol & Gloucester Opens

On 13th June, 1844 the Directors and friends made an evening trip from Bristol to Stonehouse with the locomotive *Bristol*, a six-wheeled engine, two carriages and a truck. They reached speeds of 50–60 mph. The line was opened throughout on 6th July, 1844, completing the chain of rail communication from Newcastle-on-Tyne to Exeter. Following the example of the Bristol & Exeter, a free ride was offered to every shareholder. The special train was due to leave Bristol at 10 am, but was delayed until 12.26 through the late arrival of a special from Gloucester carrying the Birmingham & Gloucester Directors. The double-headed train of 12 first and second class carriages containing about 500 passengers set off about 2½ hours late.

About two o'clock the second locomotive of this train became derailed on a sharp curve ½ mile outside Gloucester between Millstream Junction and Tramway Junction and was embedded in ballast up to its axles. Passengers walked to the banquet at the Birmingham & Gloucester station.

Brunel and Major-General Pasley, who were following the special in an inspection train, busied themselves re-railing the engine and carriages and missed the feast. The accident was caused by one of the gauge bars being bolted with only one bolt instead of several, with the result that the weight of the train spread the gauge.

In one of the speeches, Samuel Bowly, Chairman of the Birmingham line remarked that 'if the right thing had been done originally, there would have been one line throughout between Birmingham and Bristol, and there would have been no differences about broad gauge and narrow gauges'. The returning train left Gloucester 110 minutes late at 7.50 pm and arrived at Bristol at 10.15.

The line was inspected by Major-General Pasley on 6th July, 1844 with a special engine and carriage. Pasley was accompanied by Brunel, the Engineer-in-chief; Hennett, the contractor and Knapp, the contractor's solicitor. Pasley said that the bank to Staple Hill was steeper than usual, but could be surmounted by a bank engine, or a pilot engine on heavy trains, such as was on the Directors' train at the opening. Of the numerous curves, he found only 14 had a radius of less than ½ mile and the sharpest was one of 4 chains, but as this was near the Gloucester terminus, it was in a position where speeds were low. Most of the cuttings and embankments were of the favourable soil of the coal formation such as shale and not likely to slip. There were 41 overline bridges and 32 under bridges; 15 of the total of 73 were of timber. The rest were either of brick, stone, or built with stone facings and piers combined with brick arches.

There were three types of timber bridge:

(a) Wooden girder over or under bridges on stone or brick piers, which had from four to six girders, each formed from two courses of timbers one over the other and consolidated with iron plate. These beams were 9 to 10 in. in width by 26 in. deep and on them was laid 3 to 4 in. planking which supported earth and gravel if the bridge was carrying a road, or ballast and longitudinal sleepers if it carried the railway.

(b) Trussed wooden bridges over the railway which had a span of 28 ft. The two sides which served as parapets, were trussed in the form of a king post roof, but with an iron rod instead of a post. The principal parts of the truss were 10 in. square. Under the centre of the beams on each side, a transverse beam 9 in. by 18 in. was bolted up to them by means of the king post rods. Parallel to the tie beams, covering the whole space between them and flush with them at the bottom were laid longitudinal planks, 6 in. thick, with their ends resting on stone piers and their centres on the transverse beam. The two tie beams as well as the planks between them were connected by transverse iron bolts passing through them horizontally and extending the whole width of the bridge. The very unusual construction of these bridges gave them a singular appearance when viewed from the railway.

(c) Bridges of three bays of 28 ft span. Each of the two central piers consisted of a framework of five posts and a cap or dwarf brick walls. The piers at the ends of the bridge consisted of the same number of posts but rested on piles driven into the solid ground. On these piers rested six beams 9 by 18 in. and fixed to these were 4 in. planks over which the roadway of the bridge was formed of earth and gravel 1 ft deep in the centre, decreasing to 9 in. at the edges.

Pasley found 29 level crossings – 2 lanes, 22 occupation roads and 5 footpaths. When he inspected the line the stations were not finished and several miles of up line were not completed at Gloucester, but he considered a single line was not dangerous as Brunel made a rule that a pilot engine was to pass backwards and forwards, for which the regular trains had to wait.

As the Directors' train had been derailed, Pasley felt he could not pass the line, but Brunel promised that all would be right before the public opening on 8th July which had been advertised, and Pasley realised that there would be no difficulty in his fulfilling the promise. The line was opened on 8th July and Pasley made a second inspection on 10th July.

Public traffic began on 8th July with six trains running in each direction. At Gloucester trains used a temporary terminus, a platform being added to the north side of the Birmingham & Gloucester terminus, this company managing it for £500 per annum, as the GWR station had not yet been built. Excursion traffic started early and on 10th July we read of 650 teetotallers on a trip from Cheltenham to Bristol. The train was double-headed and they,

> . . . returned perfectly safe, though in the morning they experienced some delay in the journey down, from not having fixed their time of starting judiciously. At present only one line of rails has been finished for working, and it was necessary therefore for the teetotallers' special train to wait at Gloucester till the arrival of the regular morning train, so as to avoid collision. This stoppage somewhat exhausted their coal and water that they were put to some shifts for a fresh supply on their journey and the train did not reach Bristol until nearly eleven o'clock instead of about nine. The second line of rails will, it is expected, be ready for use in a few days, and then the business of the railway will go on swimmingly.

Two more excursion trains carrying from 1,400 to 1,600 passengers ran on 15th July. The first left Gloucester at 6.20 am and arrived at Bristol at 8.25. It returned from Bristol at 8 pm and arrived at Gloucester just after 10 pm. The

Bristol and Gloucester Railway.

Amalgamated with the Birmingham and Gloucester Railway.

Length 22 miles 10 chains. 8 Passenger and Goods Stations. Terminates at Temple Mead, Bristol, in junction with Great Western Railway, and at Gloucester, in junction with Birmingham and Gloucester Railway, 37½ miles in length. Passes through the counties of Gloucester and Somerset. Gauge of way, 7 feet; ruling gradients 1 in 330. Royal Assent given to Bill, 1st July, 1839. Opened throughout, 8th July, 1845. Half-yearly Meetings, March and September, at Bristol. Cost per mile, 22,700*l.* Average time of performing the journey, including stoppages, 1 hour 30 minutes. Fares throughout, First Class 8s., Second Class 5s., Third Class 3s.

Capital Account.

8,900 Shares, of 50*l.* each ; 30*l.* Paid. Whole Shares.
Total amount authorised to be raised by Shares 445,000*l.*
    Ditto   ditto   by loan or mortgage . 210,000*l.*
Total amount expended to December, 1844 . . 667,822*l.*

Cost of Working and Earnings.

Total earnings for the six months ending December, 1844 . . . . 27,544*l.*

Cost of working for the same period . . . . 19,685*l.*

Last half-yearly dividend, per share, 30s.;

(per cent., per annum. 6*l.*)

This Company have a lease of a portion of the Cheltenham and Great Western line for twenty years, at the annual rental of 18,500*l.*, to be increased 1,000*l.* per annum at the end of five years. Amalgamated with the Birmingham and Gloucester Railway, called the Bristol and Birmingham Railway Company. The united lines leased by the Midland Railway, upon payment of 6*l.* per cent. per annum on the amalgamated capital of 1,800,000*l.*

TABLE,

Shewing the PRICE of Bristol and Gloucester Railway SHARES, with the Premium or Discount thereon on the 1st January and 1st July in each of the following Years.

Amount of Share.	Amount Paid up.	Years.	Period.	Price.	Premium or Discount per Share.		In progress of Construction or Open.
					Prem.	Dis.	
50	7½	1840	July	..	..	..	In progress.
50	7½	1841	January	..	..	..	Ditto.
	9		July	..	..	..	Ditto.
50	14	1842	January	..	..	..	Ditto.
	21		July	..	..	..	Ditto.
50	24	1843	January	45	21	..	Ditto.
	30		July	53	23	..	Ditto.
50	30	1844	January	..	..	..	Ditto.
			July	..	..	..	Ditto.
50	30	1845	January	40	10	..	Open throughout.
			July	58	28	..	Ditto.

Extract from Tuck's Shareholders' Manual for 1846.

second train had passengers from Cheltenham, Tewkesbury and Worcester and was subject to 'mortifying delays', not reaching Bristol until nearly 11 am. Returning, it was delayed at Stonehouse and then subjected to a delay of a further two hours at Gloucester station. The passengers were badly treated by the Birmingham & Gloucester staff there. When asked about the delay, a Birmingham official said: 'If those fellows don't keep quiet, keep them locked in another half hour.'

A total of 4,213 passengers were carried during the first week, passengers and parcel receipts totalling £735 4s. 10d. By the week 25th–31st August, 5,427 passengers had brought in receipts of £1,122 14s. 5d. Receipts for the whole period 8th July–31st December raised an income of £27,544 2s. 6d. for 25 weeks of passenger traffic, 22 weeks of mail, 17 weeks of goods and 16 weeks of coal. The total number of passengers carried in this period was 102,937, with a total mileage of first class, 641,018; second, 1,452,472 and third 482,867, with gross receipts from passengers £18,983 15s. 10d. Total expenses in this period amounted to £11,176 13s. 7d.; locomotive and carriage charges being £6,046 2s. 2d. Deducting the extension charge payable to the Great Western and the Birmingham & Gloucester, it left a balance of £7,858 2s. 4d. and a dividend of 4 per cent was declared.

With the opening of the line, three of the six stage coaches on the route stopped running. Mails were first carried by rail on 1st August and with the opening to goods and livestock traffic on 2nd September, the break of gauge really made itself felt. The 'simple arrangement' Brunel had promised for transferring whole loads had not materialised. Coal traffic started on 9th September.

Charfield Station.

Charfield station, c.1905. A horse box stands in the dock at the far end of the down platform.   *M.J. Tozer Collection*

Chapter Four

The Bristol and Birmingham Companies Merge

Towards the end of 1844, terms of agreement for the union of the Bristol and Birmingham companies had been reached, and on 7th January, 1845, the Birmingham & Gloucester prepared a draft resolution for immediate amalgamation on the terms:

Shares of the two companies be made up:

Birmingham & Gloucester (excluding Worcester & Wolverhampton line)	1,200,000
Bristol & Gloucester	600,000
	£1,800,000

the amount to be converted into stock. 'All assets, liabilities and engagements of the two companies to be taken by the united companies.'

A Heads of Agreement was made on 14th January, 1845 between the respective Chairmen, the principal points including:

(1) The two companies to be united under the title Bristol & Birmingham Railway and an Act of Parliament to be applied for to grant powers.
(2) Until the Act is obtained, the affairs of the two companies to be administered by a board of management with 14 members – seven from each Board. The Chairman to be chosen by the Birmingham & Gloucester Board.
(3) After the passing of the Act, the Board to be elected by the proprietors of the united companies.
(4) The stock of the united company to be £1,800,000: £1,142,125 belonging to the shareholders of the Birmingham & Gloucester and £657,875 to the Bristol & Gloucester.

A Bill to constitute the Bristol & Birmingham Railway Company (B&BR) was made but withdrawn after the second reading through failure to comply with Standing Orders. In lieu of amalgamation the lines were worked as one until the Midland took over on 7th May, 1845. Immediately the agreement between the Bristol and Birmingham companies had been signed, the GWR invited them to negotiate on extending the broad gauge to Birmingham, as there was an absolute necessity for a uniform gauge from the Midlands to Bristol. These meetings resulted in a proposal to amalgamate with the Great Western. On 24th January, the GWR offered Birmingham & Gloucester shareholders £60 of GWR capital, then worth £123, for each £100 of Birmingham & Gloucester worth £109. The Bristol & Birmingham companies held out for £65 and the meeting was deferred until 27th January. On 26th January, by pure chance, John Ellis, Deputy Chairman of the Midland Railway, travelled to London in the same compartment as Edward Sturge and Joseph Gibbons, the Birmingham Directors going to the meeting. They promised him that if they did not find satisfaction with the Great Western, they would treat with him, and on his own responsibility he pledged his company to take perpetual lease of the Bristol & Birmingham at a rent of 6 per cent per annum and undertake all outstanding liabilities. On 27th January, Charles Saunders, Secretary of the GWR said that his company's offer of £60 must stand, so the Bristol & Birmingham turned to Ellis. Going to the Board of Trade to inform them of the lease, Ellis met Saunders and spoke to him, but did not tell him what he had done.

On 30th January, 1845 an agreement was officially made between Samuel Bowly, Edward Sturge and John Ellis to lease the Bristol & Birmingham. Whateley, the Birmingham & Gloucester solicitor, sent the following letter to Osborne, his Bristol counterpart:

Carlton Club, 30th January, 1845.

My dear Osborne,

The Midland Company have agreed through Mr Ellis the Deputy Chairman to take all our liabilities and to take a lease of our line from Birmingham to Bristol at 6 per cent on £1,800,000 for 14 years at least.

On Monday the agreement is to be settled, but these terms are finally agreed upon. The Great Western were previously seen by Bowly, and unhesitatingly refused to give the £65.

Yours very sincerely,

George Whateley.

A further 'Heads of Agreement' was made:

Referring to the Heads of Agreement of 14th January, 1845 for an amalgamation between the Bristol & Gloucester and Birmingham & Gloucester Companies and under the conviction of the absolute necessity of a uniformity of gauges between the northern and manufacturing districts and the Port of Bristol, it is now agreed that a lease in perpetuity of the Birmingham & Gloucester and Bristol & Gloucester shall be forthwith granted to the Midland Railway Company on the following terms:

It is understood that the amalgamation of the two first mentioned companies agreed to on the 14th January is to be considered and carried into effect.

The Midland Railway to pay to the united Birmingham and Bristol Companies an annual rent equivalent to six per cent on their united share capital of £1,800,000.

The Midland Railway Company to undertake all liabilities and engagements of the two other companies which liabilities up to the present time are estimated to amount to about £457,000.

The Stock of Engine, Carriages and all other property and effects of the Birmingham & Bristol Companies to become the property of the Midland Company.

The Midland's perpetual lease of the B&BR was to commence on 1st July. The MR had powers to purchase the two railways at any time after the expiration of three years after the commencement of the lease on payment of £150 for £100 stock. George Hudson, MR Chairman, at a meeting at Derby on 12th August, 1845 said, 'I can take no credit to myself, gentlemen, for having originated this arrangement. My friend, Mr Ellis, to whom I wish to give all the credit, which is so justly his due, suggested to the Board this bold course.'

This second amalgamation scheme rendered the first unnecessary, but it was decided to let both go before Parliament in case one failed they could fall back on the other. In 1846 there were two Bills before the House relating to the B&BR. The first was to consolidate the two companies, and this Bill was read the first time on 17th March, 1846. Two days later, 19th March, a Bill vesting the Bristol & Gloucester and the Birmingham & Gloucester in the MR was also read for the first time. On 27th March both Bills were read a second time and the former Bill was dropped. The Midland Amalgamation Act, 9–10 Vic. cap. 326 received the Royal Assent on 3rd August, 1846.

The Act stated that the share capital of the Birmingham & Gloucester Railway consisted of 9,374 shares of £100 and 8,189 of £25; the share capital of the Bristol & Gloucester was 7,539 shares of £50. The Midland could create 9,374 new shares of £100 each, 7,539 of £50, 7,539 of £37 5s. and 8,189 of £25. The Birmingham & Gloucester shareholders were to receive the same number of MR shares. Bristol & Gloucester £50 shareholders were to receive the same number of MR £50 six per cent shares and in addition, they were entitled to a like number of MR six per cent £37 5s. shares, subject to payment of that amount and 4½ per cent interest from 1st July, 1845.

The first meeting of the Bristol & Birmingham Railway was held on 14th February, 1845. Samuel Bowly was in the chair and was elected Chairman. Burgess and Harding were the joint superintendents; they had come from the Birmingham and Bristol lines respectively, and were directed to take immediate measures for working the whole route from Bristol to Birmingham as one line, and to develop its resources. The revenue from the Bristol to Gloucester section (exclusive), was to be paid into the Bristol bankers and the rest to the Birmingham bankers.

On 6th May, 1845 two Bristol Directors and two Birmingham Directors retired so that four Midland Directors could be appointed, and these four took over the entire management of the Bristol & Gloucester and Birmingham & Gloucester from 7th May, 1845. Wyndham Harding, the Bristol superintendent who had done so well for his railway, left on the same day to go to the London & Birmingham Railway.

On 7th May, 1845, the Board of Trade issued a report on the amalgamation and said: 'We are not prepared to report that we see any sufficient public reasons against allowing the proposed amalgamation of the Birmingham & Gloucester and the Bristol & Gloucester Railway companies, and the lease of the two lines to the Midland Company, in the event of Parliament being of the opinion that the extension of the narrow gauge, rather than of the wide gauge, is to be desired.'

The London & North Western Railway was anxious to keep the Great Western out of the Midlands and undertook to share any loss the Midland made by its purchase of the two railways. This aid was subsequently altered into permission for the MR to use New Street station, Birmingham, for a nominal £100 per annum. When the Midland took over the Bristol and Birmingham lines, they were not earning as much as the Midland was paying for them and in the first 18 months there was a deficit of £27,500. After this, the accounts of the lines were not kept separately, so the profitability or otherwise was not known, but a special examination at the end of 1848 showed that the lines had paid their way, and from then on were decidely profitable.

In June 1845, natural economies of the union caused the secretaryship of Robert Fletcher to be terminated, Joseph Sanders becoming Secretary of the B&BR. Brunel was asked to resign his post of Engineer, though he did not think the line in a fit state to be given up and would not relinquish his post until February 1846.

On 12th July, six months' notice was given to Stothert, Slaughter, and a month later Slaughter proposed an immediate termination of the locomotive contract. The contract was closed on 6th September, the B&BR paying him £16,000 in lieu of notice. John Cox still kept the contract to supply coke, though it was of such inferior quality that the contract was terminated on 11th May, 1846. James Edward McConnell, locomotive superintendent of the Birmingham & Gloucester Railway, was in charge of all the locomotives between Bristol and Birmingham from 6th September, 1846.

On 13–14th July, 1846 Samuel Beale, Peyton and J.H. Sanders inspected the line from Birmingham to Bristol and recommended many staffing economies. The seals of the Birmingham & Gloucester and Bristol & Gloucester, no longer being required, were destroyed at the meeting of the Board on 26th October, 1846. The last meeting of the Bristol & Birmingham Directors took place at Derby on 12th September, 1849.

In September 1846 it was suggested that it would be cheaper to use a small narrow gauge locomotive to take coal from Coalpit Heath to the junction at Westerleigh instead of paying 2d. per ton for having coal drawn from the pits by horse power. Barlow was asked to inspect the line and cause the requisite repairs to be made and notice given to the parties providing horses to discontinue them. A wooden shed to stable the horses had been built less than a year previously. The following month, Barlow reported that the best method of working this branch was to lay broad gauge rails and use a locomotive. Tenders were sought for the job of conversion and on 4th November, that of W.A. Watson to relay the branch for £1,450 was accepted. On 9th June, 1847, Barlow reported that the branch was fit for work and that the locomotive was in use.

Narrow Gauge versus Broad Gauge

The Midland Railway naturally created a fuss at having a break of gauge at Gloucester. Gooch had designed methods for transferring goods including wheels sliding on their axles and narrow gauge trucks carried on broad gauge transporter wagons, but he 'never had any faith in any of these plans working in practice'. A Royal Commission was appointed to look into the gauge question on 11th July, 1845 and evidence began on 6th August. When the Parliamentary Gauge Committee visited Gloucester, J.D. Payne, goods manager of the Birmingham & Gloucester and later general manager of the South Staffordshire Railway, arranged for two trains already dealt with, to be unloaded to add to the work, so that the chaos the break of gauge caused would be more impressive. Matters were not helped by the inadequate transfer shed which was far too small for the volume of traffic it was required to handle.

G.P. Neele wrote in *Railway Reminiscences*:

> When the members came to the scene, they were appalled by the clamour arising from the well-arranged confusion of shouting out addresses of consignments, the chucking of packages across from truck to truck, the enquiries for missing articles, the loading, unloading and reloading, which his clever device [sic] had brought into operation.

The Great Western thought that the Commission should have seen the break of gauge at Bristol, not Gloucester, as it was against the B&BR's interest for things to have gone smoothly. The Midland had a good case, however, because narrow gauge to Bristol would have greatly reduced transhipment. In the week ending 25th October, 1845, almost 700 tons were transhipped at Gloucester and only 50 tons at Bristol, with a weekly average of 200–300 tons at Gloucester and 40 tons at Bristol. Another saving would have been in locomotives, for their narrow gauge engine stock would have sufficed and the number of turntables, engine sheds and goods sheds could have been reduced by half. The transfer of goods at Gloucester took an average of 50 minutes for a 5-ton wagon and cost a maximum of 3d. a ton. Nineteen extra porters had to be employed as a consequence of the transhipment and the B&BR estimated that the break of gauge cost them £2,000 a year. Some items, such as meat, deteriorated due to delays in transhipment between the gauges.

J.E. McConnell giving evidence before the Gauge Commission said, regarding passengers:

> We have tried to lessen this inconvenience . . . passengers leave their carriage of either gauge and walk round under the shed to the other side where a 'broad' . . . or 'narrow' train stands. The luggage is put into little barrows and conveyed round with them. Delays are, of course, inevitable, but passengers are under cover all the time. We must admit there is great inconvenience to invalids . . . Delay is never less than fifteen minutes and often more if carriages and horses have to be transhipped; then the delay is as much as half an hour for an eight coach train.

Wyndham Harding added:

> The result of a delay with the Mail trains for instance . . . is sometimes just sufficient . . . to miss the Manchester, or other train from Birmingham, or the Exeter or Bath train from Bristol; annoyance to the passengers who were anxious about their parcels and packages; risk and expense, as a large body of porters have [sic] to be retained who are not fully occupied [between trains], in order that no more time than is necessary should be lost in the change of trains.

It was relatively easy for passengers from Bristol to Birmingham to change trains as they simply stepped across the platform, specially increased in width from 12 ft to 22 ft in 1844 to cope with the transfer traffic, straight into a narrow gauge train. However, it was a very different story for those in the other direction as this involved trudging from the Birmingham & Gloucester arrival platform, situated at the southern part of the station complex, to the B&GR departure platform on the northern side of the station, and all along platforms only ten to twelve feet in width. Matters were not helped by the fact that the Birmingham & Gloucester Railway, the B&GR and the GWR all using the same station, used Birmingham, Bristol and London time respectively, so Gloucester station had three clocks set at three different times which added to the confusion. Matters were even further complicated when B&GR trains departed, as they frequently did, from their arrival platform!

Broad gauge supporters fixed a poster at Gloucester:

Observe – Petition! Petition 50 miles an hour versus 25. Coaches before waggons – the blessing of the broad gauge for the Northern districts. Safety and speed before cramp and delay. Advancement before retreat. The petition will be ready in a day or two. Brunel for ever! Hurrah!

Another placard said it took 1 hour 45 minutes between Bristol and Gloucester on the broad gauge, a distance of 37 miles, and 2 hours 35 minutes for the 51 miles between Gloucester and Birmingham on the narrow gauge. On the broad gauge, it pointed out, passengers had 'a large and commodious carriage for their accommodation', but were 'cribbed, crowded, cramped and confined and nearly stifled' in a small and inconvenient narrow gauge carriage.

In January 1840 the B&GR had proposed building an independent line between Standish and Gloucester, and in 1845 the Bristol & Birmingham lodged a Bill for such a line. It was read for the third time on 6th July, 1846, but was suspended by Parliament pending the report of the Gauge Commission. On 19th June, 1846 the Board of Trade recommended that broad gauge should be kept between Bristol and Gloucester, but that narrow gauge should be laid within the broad gauge line. At a shareholders' meeting held on 6th March, 1847, it was decided that narrow gauge should be built from Gloucester to Bristol, but the scheme was postponed pursuant to a resolution of the House of Lords of 10th June, 1847. Finally, on 14th August, 1848, the Act 11 & 12 Vic. cap. 131, allowed the Midland to build an independent line from Gloucester to Stonehouse and mixed gauge to Bristol. The Act allowed £110,000 to be raised and the work had to be completed within seven years. The narrow gauge metals to Bristol were first used on 22nd May, 1854.

Herapath's Journal reported on 27th May, 1854:

On Monday, May 22, the narrow gauge line between Gloucester and Bristol was opened to the public. Passengers will be able to proceed direct from the north to Bristol without change of carriage, while some 10 to 15 minutes' time formerly occupied in shifting passengers' luggage will be saved. A considerable saving will be effected by the company in the goods department, as every parcel and package conveyed from the north to the south had to be moved from a narrow gauge to a broad gauge truck.

With the abolition of broad gauge on the Midland Railway, its redundant stock was advertised for sale by auction at Gloucester in May 1856. It consisted of:

    7 first class carriages
    5 composites
    6 second class
    6 third class
    3 carriage trucks
    3 horse boxes
    1 passenger engine
    1 goods engine
   29 high-sided wagons
    8 low-sided timber wagons
    1 6-wheeled timber truck

In the event no stock was sold, as no bidder appeared, so Kirtley was authorised to offer it to Brassey, the contractor, for the lowest price the company was justified at selling it. In June, 13 broad gauge coaches were sold to the Bristol & Exeter Railway for £1,300, while the following month Brassey bought one broad gauge engine for £1,000.

Now having its own tracks from Standish to Gloucester, the Midland ceased using the Great Western metals and tried unsuccessfully to set aside the 1843 agreement, but had to continue to pay tolls for a line it did not use, until 12th May, 1865 when the twenty years' obligation came to an end.

Because of the Midland Amalgamation Act, broad gauge rails had to remain between Bristol and Standish although never used by the GWR. The Act, upholding the 1843 agreement, required the Midland to maintain between Bristol and Standish 'two lines of railway on the same gauge as the Great Western Railway' and permit them to pass 'at all reasonable and proper times'. Broad gauge rails were removed in 1872 when all lines in the Gloucester district were converted, but a Bristol & Exeter train still ran to Parkfield colliery until January 1882. The GWR ran goods trains from Gloucester to Bristol over the Midland route from 1st August, 1871 until the opening of the Severn Tunnel, and also found these running powers useful in 1908 for the Wolverhampton to Bristol express.

Royalty too had to contend with the inconvenience of changing gauge at Gloucester. Queen Victoria is seen here crossing from the Birmingham & Gloucester's narrow gauge train in the background, to the Bristol & Gloucester's broad gauge train in the foreground, 29th September, 1849.   *Courtesy Illustrated London News*

Following the withdrawal of the passenger service to Bath in March 1966 and a general reduction in traffic, coupled with the need for rationalisation in connection with resignalling in the Bristol area, the line from Lawrence Hill Junction to Mangotsfield North Junction was declared redundant and closed on 29th December, 1969, trains running from Yate to Temple Meads using the former GWR route via Filton. This closure was a few days earlier than planned due to a 40 ft long section of a 20 ft high embankment breaking away at the lorry park, Thicket Road, Staple Hill. Only the up line from Mangotsfield North Junction to Yate was retained for use by trains carrying coal to Bath gas works, the down main from Mangotsfield North Junction to the 120¼ mile post being retained as an engineer's siding for track machine operator training.

When the Yate South Junction to Bath line closed on 31st May, 1971, rails from Mangotsfield to Yate South Junction were retained for engineer's use. This line subsequently closed south of 122 miles 65 chains at the point where a bridge carries the M4 motorway across the track making a 'shed' for permanent way vehicles. On 19th November, 1985 Avon County Council opened a refuse terminal on part of the site of Westerleigh Up Sidings. Here containers of rubbish are loaded on to rail for transport to a landfill site at Calvert, Buckinghamshire. To the south of this, a Murco Oil Distribution Terminal was opened on 1st March, 1991.

The former track bed lay dormant following lifting of the permanent way, but then in 1986 the Mangotsfield to St Philip's section was returned to use as part of the Bristol & Bath Railway Path. This 20 km long route for pedestrians, cyclists, and wheelchair users, was the first major project of its kind. in Britain. The cutting sections which nature has reclaimed, in particular, give an almost rural aspect within Bristol, while passing through Staple Hill Tunnel offers a measure of excitement. For the hundreds of daily commuters using the Mangotsfield to St Philip's section, the path has opened up new views of the city and enables them to reach the City Centre in approximately 25 minutes by a traffic-free route. A special feature of the path is a series of sponsored sculptures at points of interest. Most are dual-purpose, serving as seats or drinking fountains, in addition to being works of art. At the time of writing, plans are being formulated to extend the path from Mangotsfield to Yate.

MIDLAND RAILWAY Co. G F 155

____ —/ 189

FROM AVONSIDE WHARF STATION, BRISTOL,

To _West Pennard_

Company _S & D_

Route _Bath_

Wagon No. _Taylar_

Consignee _Taylar & Hooker_

Chapter Five

Railways Associated with the Bristol & Gloucester

In 1843 the Bristol & Gloucester subscribed £50,000 towards the £400,000 capital of the South Devon Railway and in the following year co-operated with the Great Western, Bristol & Exeter and South Devon in forming the Cornwall Railway and subscribed £25,000 towards it.

On 7th December, 1842 the Gloucester & Dean Forest Railway proposed a 12-mile line to link the Bilson area with Gloucester and had this scheme come to fruition, it would have formed a junction with the Birmingham & Gloucester, Bristol & Gloucester and C&GWUR. Another abortive scheme was one planned by Brunel, the South Wales & South of Ireland Railway, which was to run from Stonehouse, but met great opposition as it left out Gloucester and all the large Monmouthshire towns. The following year the Wilts & Glos Railway was proposed, to run from a junction with the B&GR at Stonehouse to Thingley Junction, near Chippenham, on the Great Western Bristol to London line. This proposal too proved abortive. Also, on 15th July, 1845, a report of the Select Sub-Committee of the Kennet & Avon Canal made an abortive proposal for a line from Bath to the B&GR.

Hardly associated, but a rival line to the B&GR, was the Gloucester & Bristol Railway surveyed by John Hawkshaw in 1836 under the direction of Walker & Burges, engineers. It saved nearly 3 miles compared with the B&GR, had a ruling gradient of 1 in 300 instead of 1 in 73 and had a shorter length of tunnelling. It was to start from Bristol Harbour, immediately west of the Coalpit Heath line (a branch led to the Great Western at Temple Meads), and run to Castle Green where a station was to be built over the River Frome. Like the B&GR it was intended to join the C&GWUR at Stonehouse; the Gloucester & Bristol line was to have a triangular junction there. A modified scheme was put forward by the same promoters the following year.

Later Branches

In the latter half of the nineteenth century, quite a number of branches were built from the B&GR. The Dursley Railway, which left the main line at Coaley, was opened on 18th September, 1856, and the Stonehouse to Nailsworth branch on 1st February, 1867. From Dudbridge on this latter line, a branch was opened to Stroud on 16th November, 1885. On 4th August, 1869 a line from Mangotsfield to Bath was opened, and when the Somerset & Dorset Railway arrived at Bath on 20th July, 1874, this gave the Midland Railway an important through route to the London & South Western Railway and the south coast.

The Yate to Thornbury branch was opened on 2nd September, 1872 and on 1st October, 1874, a line from Kingswood Junction, Bristol, to Clifton Down via the Clifton Joint Railway. On 24th February, 1877, this line was extended to Sneyd Park Junction giving access to Avonmouth over the Bristol Port Railway & Pier. A branch to Sharpness was opened on 2nd August, 1875, and this grew in importance when the Severn Bridge was opened on 17th October, 1879. On 9th March, 1908, the Berkeley loop was

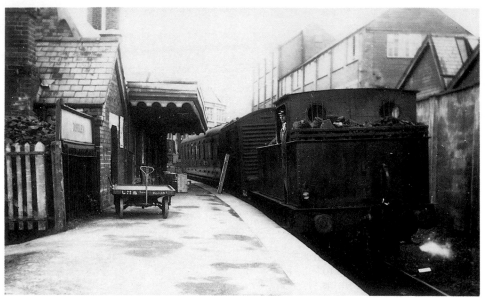

No. 41727 on the branch service seen here at Dursley station in September, 1951.

H.C. Casserley

Thornbury station buildings photographed on 25th August, 1956.   *R.M. Casserley*

opened, giving the Great Western a through run from the Severn Bridge to their new South Wales & Bristol Direct line at Westerleigh.

Besides opening up access to the Forest of Dean and the docks at Sharpness, the Great Western envisaged other advantages. When the Severn Tunnel needed to be closed for repair, trains could be diverted via the new Berkeley Road and Westerleigh Loop, while another bonus was that with the opening of the new line from Birmingham & Cheltenham on 1st August, 1906, the GWR had a direct route from Birmingham to Bristol. It could use its own track from Birmingham to Standish Junction and then its running powers over the Midland Railway to Yate to regain its own metals via the Westerleigh Loop.

On 1st July, 1908, the GWR inaugurated a new express between Wolverhampton and Bristol, the first train being hauled each way by the new 'Flower' class 4–4–0 No. 4101 *Auricula*. The route of this express was contested by the Midland Railway which claimed that the Westerleigh Loop was only authorised as a route to Sharpness and the Severn Bridge, and not to facilitate competition between Birmingham and Bristol. It held that the new train must keep to the Midland lines all the way into Bristol, paying toll for the extra ten miles. This the Great Western had to do until November, invariably finding that a slow stopping train was in the long block sections just ahead of the new express.

In October the Court of Appeal reversed judgement and from the 2nd November, 1908 the GWR was able to use its own line from Westerleigh to Bristol. The Midland still countered the GWR's competition by refusing to allow the larger Great Western locomotives over Stonehouse viaduct, this meaning that the GWR had to use its smaller engines, the 4–4–0 'Counties'.

Nailsworth station buildings photographed on 25th August, 1956.   *R.M. Casserley*

Bristol Temple Meads: a down MR express headed by a 2−4−0 (probably No. 253). The view taken is from the footbridge; a GWR corridor train stands on the left.

M.J. Tozer Collection

Chapter Six

Description of the Line

The Bristol & Gloucestershire started at Cuckold's Pill on the Floating Harbour, Bristol, later Avon Street* Wharf. A branch led to the company's yard, later to become St Philip's station, near the top of Old Market.

Prior to 1858 the inwards and outwards goods departments of the MR at Bristol were carried on in the GWR's Temple Meads goods depot, but that year, because of an increase in traffic, the MR inwards goods department moved to the MR coal yard at St Philip's where a goods depot was erected and eight years later was doubled in size to accommodate the outwards department as well. The building, erected by Humphries of Derby, measured 180 ft × 133 ft and was supported on cast iron columns resting on wrought iron girders. Fifteen hydraulic cranes of Sir William Armstrong's patent pattern lifted up to two tons, and were so placed that as one lifted goods from the trucks to the platform, another lifted goods from the platform to the trucks on the other side. Six traversing tables were worked by hydraulic power. Hydraulic capstan engines capable of moving 80 tons drew wagons in or out of the shed. Hydraulic power came from an Armstrong patent accumulator worked by two engines of about 60 hp.

A feature of the shed, adopted from St Pancras passenger station, was that below were spacious cellars for the storage of over 15,000 hogsheads of Burton and other ales consigned to tradesmen in the neighbourhood, a new facility which the company had recently developed. The building also stabled 50 horses belonging to the MR, while nearby were the corn lofts. The yard had 20 roads. A carriage dock permitted horse-drawn furniture vans and other wheeled vehicles to be loaded and discharged, while extensive cattle pens and coal yards adjoined. Trace horses were required to assist hauling heavy loads up the short, steep slope from the goods depot. It was badly damaged during the blitz in World War II, the overall roof of the shed being destroyed.

The 'LMS Goods Stations & Depots in Bristol' book published in 1926 said that St Philip's had a commodious goods shed with up-to-date electric and hydraulic cranes for the handling and quick despatch of general goods traffic, while in addition there was extensive outside accommodation with sidings and cranes capable of lifting up to 20 tons.

Oil gas for carriage lighting and restaurant car cooking was made at Barrow Road carriage sidings, but the gas works closed in 1934 and supplies were then obtained from the GWR at an annual saving of £350. This amount was divided in equal proportion between the LMSR and GWR in accordance with the agreed pooling and closer working arrangements.

An engine drew coaches from St Philip's carriage sidings to Lawrence Hill Junction, then reversed the whole train into Temple Meads Old Station about a mile distant, pushing 12 coaches in reverse over busy junctions, with just a shunter in the leading coach giving hand signals – a highly unsatisfactory arrangement.

The single platform, timber-built St Philip's passenger station (129 miles 63 chains from Derby) with ridge and furrow roof, opened on 2nd May, 1870 to ease congestion at Temple Meads, mainly taking trains to and from the

---

* or Avonside

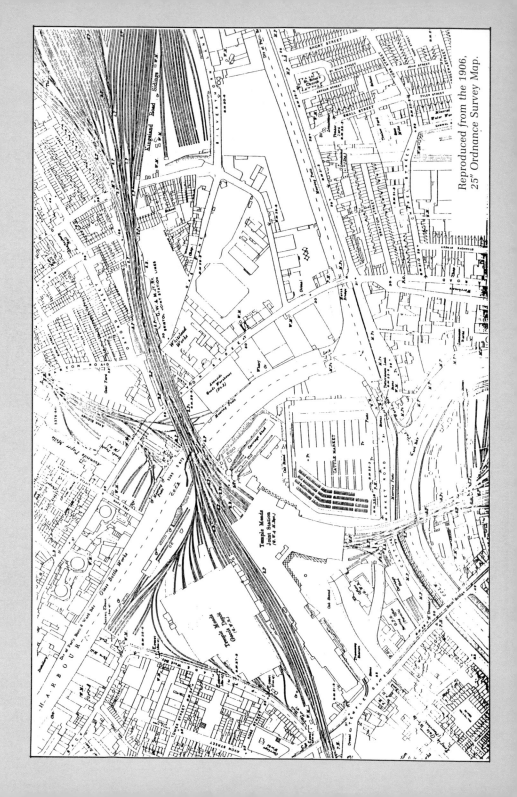

Reproduced from the 1906, 25" Ordnance Survey Map.

Avon Street level crossing looking towards St Philip's from Avonside Wharf on 1st April, 1954.

Dr A.J.G. Dickens/Author's Collection

A crane unloading a barrel from MR barge No. 5 at Avonside Wharf into William Butler's tar barrel wagon, c.1910. *Author's Collection*

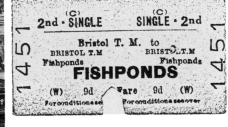

The site of St Philip's Goods Depot, now occupied by Avon County Council's Great Western Refuse Transfer Station, looking towards Avonside Wharf on 17th March, 1990. *Author*

St Philip's station, view towards the stop blocks, 16th September, 1953.
Dr A.J.G. Dickens/Author's Collection

Bath branch, opened the previous year. Following the enlargement of Temple Meads in the 1930s, it closed on 21st September, 1953, a gas leak causing an explosion which destroyed part of the station shortly before it shut.

Avonside Wharf, just over a quarter of a mile distant from St Philip's goods depot, had an extensive water frontage and electric, steam and hydraulic cranes for loading or discharging barges. A covered dock allowed traffic to be transferred from barge to railway wagon fully protected from the weather. Nearby were very commodious warehouses. The MR, and later the LMS, kept a local fleet of barges. Following the closure of the former Midland line in 1969, a new chord line was opened from the former GWR station at Lawrence Hill to give access to the Wharf.

The Wharf Branch closed in 1990, but the northern section is still used by trains to the Avon County Council's curiously named Great Western Refuse Transfer Station at Barrow Road, built on part of the site of the Midland Railway's St Philip's goods yard and locomotive depot. Here, five days a week, containers of rubbish are placed on rail and taken to Calvert, Buckinghamshire.

The very busy Lawrence Hill Junction signal box, controlling St Philip's Yard and Barrow Road Locomotive Depot in addition to the main line to and from Temple Meads, was manned by two signalmen and a booking boy. Beyond, the line climbed at 1 in 55–114 for 2¼ miles to Kingswood Junction where the branch from Avonmouth and Clifton Down joined. Quite a few trains were banked from Folly Lane Bridge, south of the engine depot, to Fishponds, class '4F' 0–6–0s being mainly used for this work. A banking engine was kept opposite Engine Shed Sidings signal box and although passenger trains requiring assistance were supposed to stop, this did not always happen in practice and it was not unknown for a signalman to let out a banker on to the main line to catch up and assist up the gradient. The gradient caused a restriction of not more than 4½ vehicles to be carried behind the rear brake van of a passenger train. Beside the banker siding was a coal stack, originally laid down by Italian prisoners-of-war in World War II to whom time was no object and it had an unusually neat appearance.

Trains requiring to shunt traffic at Bristol Wagon Works sidings were required to carry the train staff kept in Lawrence Hill Junction signal box.

Fishponds, (127 miles 9 chains) not opened until 1st April, 1866, was originally 'Stapleton', being renamed 'Fish Ponds' on 1st January, 1867 and made a single word on 1st May, 1939. Built of brick and stone, the station housed the Bristol District Control Office. A ridge and furrow roof covered the up platform. A bay platform on the down side was provided for Clifton Down and Avonmouth trains, though latterly was mainly used by bankers and light engines awaiting clearance to proceed to Barrow Road shed. The sharp Bristol & Gloucestershire Railway curve west of the station was eased when the line was converted to broad gauge.

Fishponds was a busy station dealing with china clay for the potteries and considerable coal traffic, the Bottom Yard dealing with fuel for Fishponds Coal Company, and the Top Yard with coal for various other merchants.

Fishponds, looking in the down direction, *c*.1910.   *Author's Collection*

Fishponds, a view in the up direction, 21st April, 1960.   *Author*

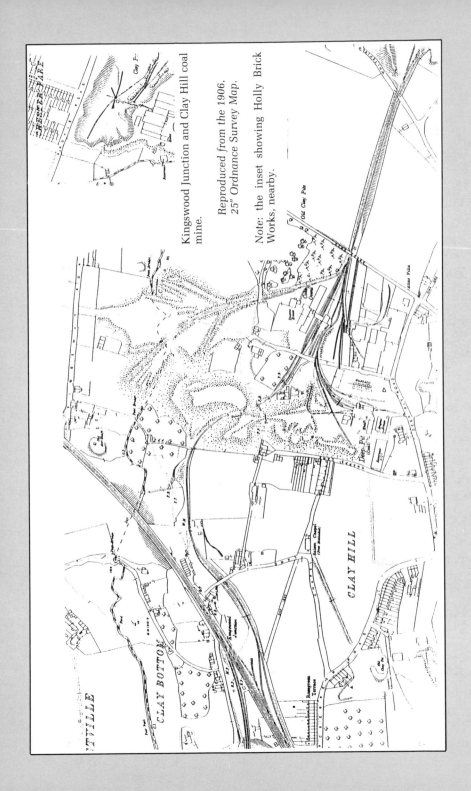

Kingswood Junction and Clay Hill coal mine.

Reproduced from the 1906, 25" Ordnance Survey Map.

Note: the inset showing Holly Brick Works, nearby.

A siding led to Peckett & Sons locomotive building works. This line was shared with Kingswood Colliery until coal winding ceased on 3rd April, 1936. The colliery locomotive also shunted for the locomotive works, but between 1936 and 1958, *Nancy*, a Peckett 0–6–0ST hauled new, or repaired, engines in and out. The last locomotive left the works in February 1962.

The climb continued, but flattened for a short distance to 1 in 583 between Fishponds and Staple Hill (126 miles 34 chains). Staple Hill station opened on 1st November, 1888 and had its offices at street level, with a wooden waiting room on the platform near the foot of a zig-zag path, while additionally there was a small ticket office on the down platform. Unlike most of the other stations on the line, it was not a block post. In the 1930s Staple Hill was well-used by commuters, some walking from Downend and others from the Mangotsfield side of Staple Hill tunnel. Although the electric trams, which ran from Staple Hill to Old Market, were readily accessible, they were more expensive than a railway season ticket.

Staple Hill tunnel was 515 yds long and originally 12 ft in width, but was widened to 26 ft on the north side by the Bristol & Gloucester. Like the bridges, it was never full broad gauge width. The two shafts used in its excavation were left open for light; today, because of its original single line construction, the shafts are over the site of the down line. The tunnel's first 264 yds were on a rising gradient of 1 in 800, the remainder being level. Its section was,

> . . . an oblong [sic] segment of a circle, having an extreme width of 28 ft, with an extreme height of 24 ft above the level of the rails; the side walls being of pennant stone 2 ft thick and the arch generally composed of five half-brick rings, chiefly laid in cement. In some portions, measuring 42 yds in length, where the soil was not satisfactory, inverted brick arches 18 in. thick have been formed, having a span of 26 ft and a versed sine of 1½ ft.

North and south of the tunnel, the cutting has a wall only on the west side, further evidence of subsequent widening.

Beyond the tunnel was a sharp curve where the line skirted Rodway Hill. Keynsham Junction with the Avon & Gloucestershire Railway was on the site of the later Mangotsfield North Junction. A weighbridge and toll house were here to keep an account of all coal going to the Avon. The Bristol & Gloucester Railway built a station house which was separated from the platforms when in March 1845 the Board resolved 'that a station on the cheapest scale be established at Mangotsfield.' It was opened shortly after and in 1848 was improved by having a shed for passengers waiting for up trains. This original Mangotsfield station was closed to passenger traffic when the Bath branch was opened on 4th August, 1869, and a new, more suitable junction station built ½ mile to the south, at the apex of the junction of the Gloucester and Bath lines. An up and down main platform was provided for each line, with a down bay platform for passenger trains running between Mangotsfield and Clifton Down, and an up loop platform on the Gloucester line. These roads were known as 'behind the box' and 'under the rock' respectively, the former receiving its name from the signal box, and the latter from Rodway Hill which dominated the station. A tall

The Fishponds station master seated, *centre*, with his staff around him, *c.*1922. The hoarding has posters advertising Borwick's baking powder; Cerebos salt, Puritan soap and Foster Clark's custard.   *Author's Collection*

Girls from Carson's Chocolate Factory bid farewell to troops from the Beaufort War Hospital, Fishponds during World War I. The soldiers had been entertained at Carson's.   *Courtesy Downend Local History Society*

Class '4F' 0−6−0 No. 44263 emerges from the 513 yards-long Staple Hill tunnel into Staple Hill station with a down freight on 21st April, 1960. The station building has timber walls, set on a low brick wall. Notice the intermediate signal (at the end of the platform) worked from Fishponds signal box. *Author*

Staple Hill, looking in the down direction. The wire from Fishponds signal box to work the up intermediate signal can be seen below the platform edging, also gas pipes to feed the platform lamps. Photographed *c*.1960. *Lens of Sutton*

timber screen adjacent to the down bay, protected the station to some extent from the prevailing westerly winds. Platform No. 1, 'under the rock' was mainly used for parcel and pigeon traffic; platforms Nos. 2 and 3 were to and from Gloucester; platforms Nos. 4 and 5 were to and from Bath, while No. 6 was the bay platform. The Rodway Hill Golf Club was one of the most popular around Bristol and quite a number of members travelled direct by train from Clifton Down.

The platforms at Mangotsfield were covered by glazed roofing supported by lightweight girders on slender cast iron columns. The roof was longitudinal in construction, rather than the normal Midland ridge-and-furrow type, its ends hipped and carrying small finials. The island platforms had timber waiting shelters. The platforms were connected by subway and it is said that when this was being cut circa 1900, enough coal was extracted from the outcrop for the labourers to boil their tea. The dark, dank subway inspired the Bath playwright Arnold Ridley to write 'The Ghost Train'. The fact that the station lacked a refreshment room has been explained by the story that the landowner, who also had land on which was sited the nearest hotel, stipulated that the railway could have the land as long as no refreshment facilities were offered.

In addition to being used as a junction station for passengers changing trains, and for passengers to or from Mangotsfield itself, it was also adjacent to Carson's chocolate factory, which had a large number of employees, some of whom travelled by rail. Douglas motor cycles could be seen in wooden crates on the passenger platforms, the machines being built in the area. Farmers brought churns of milk for despatch. The station closed to passengers on 7th March, 1966 when passenger services on the Bath branch were withdrawn. Curiously for a principal junction station, it had but one water crane and this was tucked away on a siding by the down main line signal. The staff consisted of a station master; two booking clerks; two foremen; three porters on each of two daily shifts and one night porter.

Mangotsfield station signal box, named South Junction until 29th October, 1877, was destroyed by fire on 22nd January, 1967, but not replaced, the curve between the station and the new Mangotsfield South Junction being closed on that date. South of the station were engineer's sidings on the down side and a private siding, access to which was given (from 10th December, 1877) by Mangotsfield Stone Sidings signal box; this closed on 21st July, 1935. The siding on the up side south of the station was known as Tar Pot Siding. Mail was collected from a pick-up arm on the Gloucester side of the station, a postman pushing a trolley from the village post office.

The two goods sidings at Mangotsfield North were shunted by Bristol men, these also working Carson's private siding, opened in 1912 as Packer's, and closed in 1963. Crews shunting this siding were allowed to purchase chocolates at a reduced rate. The goods depot at Mangotsfield North closed on 10th June, 1963, though the old station house remains. The first building was the small one storey toll house built in 1830 for the Avon & Gloucestershire and Bristol & Gloucestershire railways, with the two storey station house built beside it in 1844. Mangotsfield North goods sidings were used to hold wagons of coal for Stapleton Road Gas Works if Westerleigh Yard was

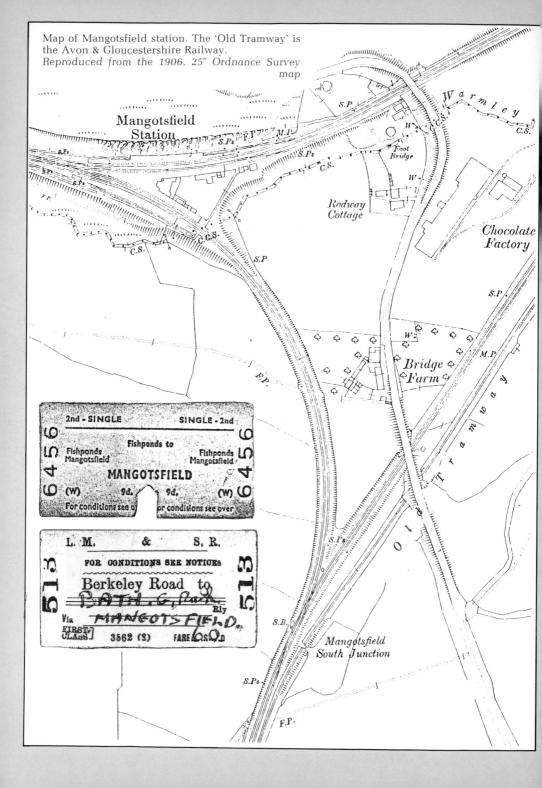

Map of Mangotsfield station. The 'Old Tramway' is the Avon & Gloucestershire Railway.
Reproduced from the 1906, 25" Ordnance Survey map

Class '2P' 4–4–0 No. 504 heads an up express at Mangotsfield, *c.*1920. Notice the
burnished buffers on the engine.   *Miles Davey*

A fine view of Mangotsfield station platform awnings in April 1950. The view is
facing Bristol.   *H.C. Casserley*

Mangotsfield old station house at North Junction, with the original single storey weighbridge house to the right. 11th May, 1967. *Author*

The 9.20 Bristol to Gloucester headed by 4—4—0, No. 1073 local service seen here approaching Mangotsfield on 5th July, 1947. *H.C. Casserley*

A down stopping train at Mangotsfield hauled by class '2P' 4—4—0 No. 528. The gradient post by the Bath branch platform shows 'Level/1 in 168'. The nameboard high under the nearest canopy reads: 'Mangotsfield Junction for Gloucester, Worcester, Birmingham and the North', while that beyond says, 'Mangotsfield Junction for Bath and the Somerset & Dorset Line'. *Miles Davey*

Westerleigh sidings, looking in the up direction on 21st April, 1960. The wagon repair depot can be seen at the far left.   *Author*

Westerleigh oil terminal on the site of the former marshalling yard.   *Author*

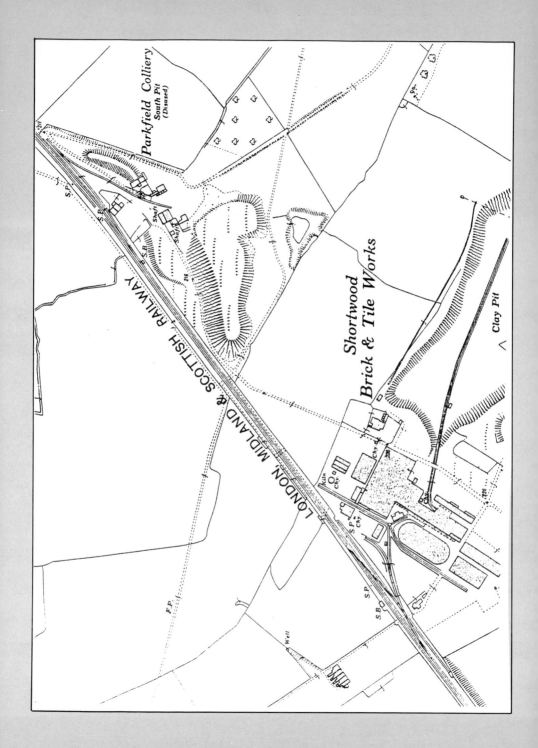

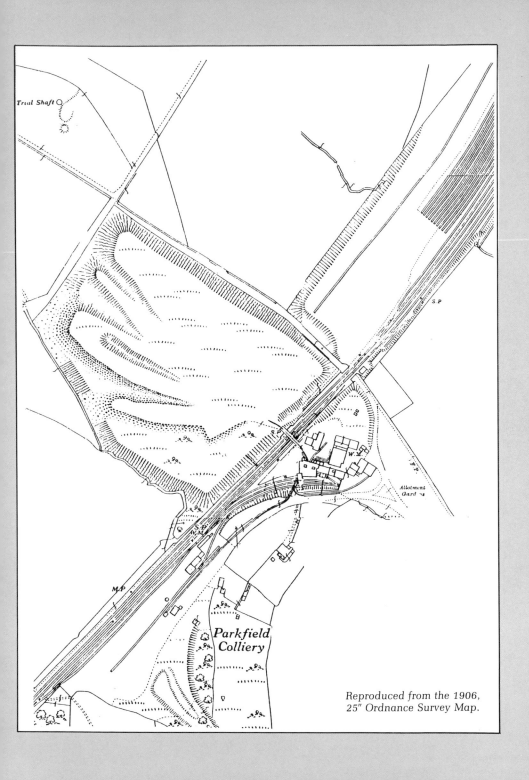

Trial Shaft

S.P

W.M.

Allotment
Gard

S.P
W.M.

M.P

*Parkfield
Colliery*

Reproduced from the 1906,
25″ Ordnance Survey Map.

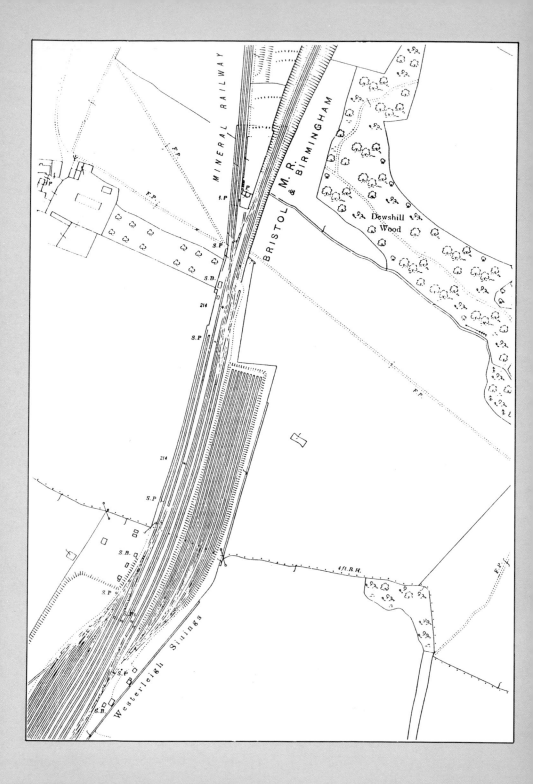

Permanent Way track machine DX7 3414 approaches the site of Westerleigh Yard from the north, on what was the main line from Gloucester, on 1st March, 1991.

Author

Class '60' No. 033 *Anthony Ashley Cooper* tests the track with an empty tanker car on 1st March, 1991. *Author*

too full to store them. Opposite the North Junction signal box were three carriage sidings; these were taken out of use on 12th September, 1965, the box itself closing on 3rd January, 1970. In the 1960s the rotted window frames in the MR box were replaced by those of GWR pattern. *Circa* 1940/1 a bomb fell in the 'four foot' at North Junction halting all traffic through to Bristol.

On the down side north of Shortwood Bridge, coal seams were opened up when clearing the slopes of a cutting, tempting one permanent way man to take some home to burn. Shortwood brick works specialised in making engineering bricks for bridges, tunnels and mines, two-thirds of its output going to South Wales. Shortwood signal box, with just a home and distant in each direction, was closed at night and during World War II was worked by a signalwoman. A little further north were the sidings of Shortwood coal works and Parkfield Colliery, opened in 1856.

Westerleigh Marshalling Yard, proposed in 1898 and opened 1900–1 to ease congestion at Bath and Bristol, consisted of 13 up and 12 down roads. Both Westerleigh Up and Down Sidings signal boxes had mostly point, rather than signal, levers. The men on duty had to keep pulling levers for shunting movements and sometimes did not even have a rest during the shunters' lunch break if the Yard Inspector took over shunting. The first diesel locomotive in the area shunted at Westerleigh c.1956. From Westerleigh Yard, a mile long branch led to Coalpit Heath, the last colliery in that group closing in 1950, but part of the line was retained for wagon storage until 1956. The branch had its own locomotives, one, *Lord Salisbury* ending its days at Norton Hill Colliery on the Somerset & Dorset Railway at Midsomer Norton. Westerleigh Yard closed on 19th January, 1965, part of the site being re-developed 20 years later as Avon County Council's Westerleigh Refuse Terminal from where containers are sent to Calvert, Buckinghamshire.

On 1st March, 1991 another part of the site was opened as an oil distribution depot for Murco Petroleum. Products arrive in 100 tonne rail tankers, the depot being capable of handling 32 cars at a time. A gantry above each of the two tracks provides both lighting and a handrail for people walking or working on top of the tankers. As a fire precaution, after pushing the tank cars into the sidings, a locomotive waits outside the compound before collecting the empty wagons after they have been discharged.

The summit of the B&GR was at Beech Hill, south of Yate, not far from Yate South Junction. The GWR's Wootton Bassett to Filton line, opened in 1903, passed over the MR by a three-arch stone bridge, though at first the contractors used a temporary wooden structure. The junctions at Yate were mentioned in Chapter Five. For a distance of 1½ miles the up line between Westerleigh Junction and Yate has been adapted for reversible working for Amey Roadstone Company traffic from Tytherington Quarry on the former Thornbury branch, to give access to the Stoke Gifford Down Yard, though at the time of writing, the train service on this branch is 'as required'. This reversible line was also used as a passing loop on at least one occasion, for on 26th August, 1972 the 8.45 am Liverpool to Penzance used it to overtake the 9.30 am Nottingham to Paignton which had got ahead of its path by

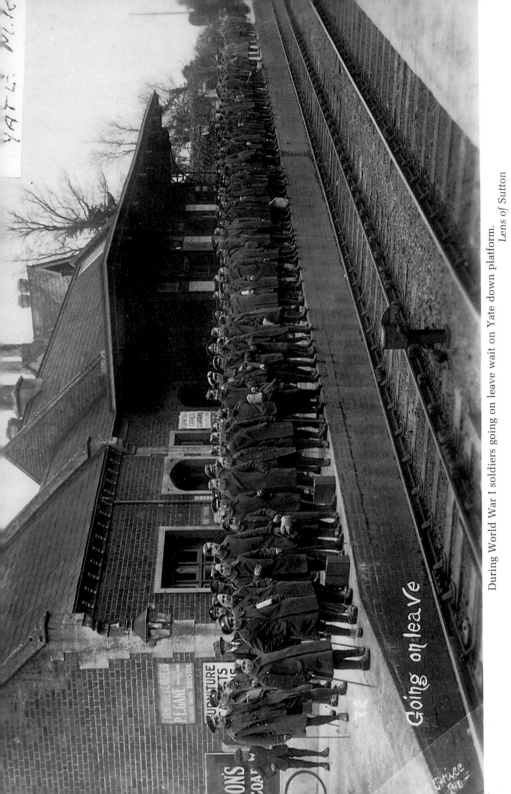

Going on leave

During World War I soldiers going on leave wait on Yate down platform.

Lens of Sutton

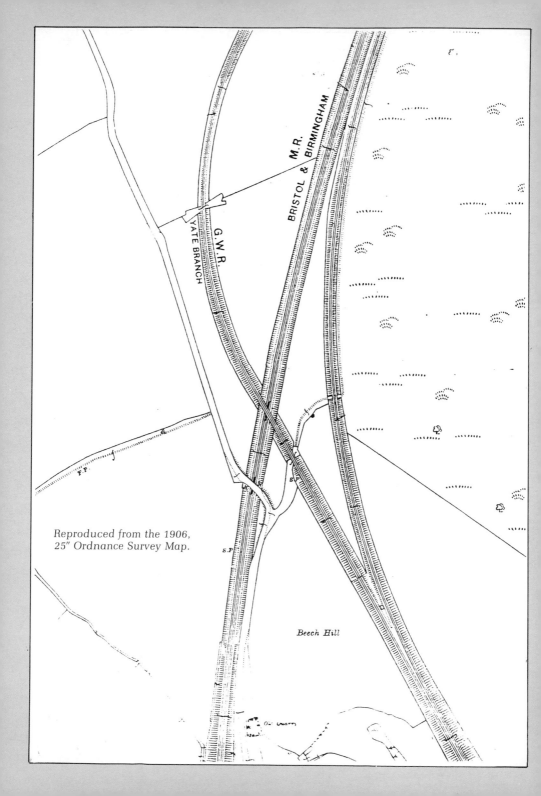

M.R.

BRISTOL & BIRMINGHAM

G.W.R.

YATE BRANCH

F.P.

S.P.

S.P.

Beech Hill

Reproduced from the 1906, 25" Ordnance Survey Map.

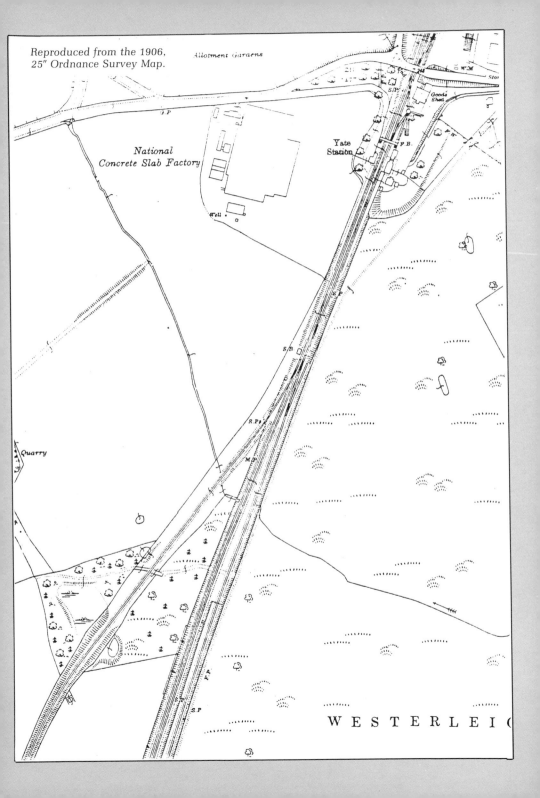

Reproduced from the 1906,
25″ Ordnance Survey Map.

Allotment Gardens

*National
Concrete Slab Factory*

G.P

Well

Yate
Station

S.B.

Goods
Shed

F.B.

S.P.

M.P.

Quarry

S.P.

W E S T E R L E I

Yate station captured in the sunlight on 25th September, 1960 looking towards
Gloucester.

R.M. Casserley

Yate looking in the up direction, 11th May, 1961. Notice the Brunellian architecture.

Author

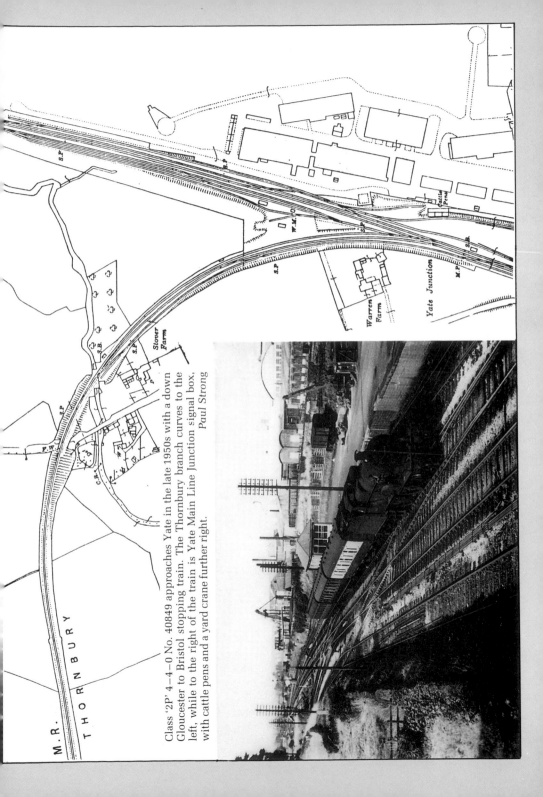

Class '2P' 4–4–0 No. 40849 approaches Yate in the late 1950s with a down Gloucester to Bristol stopping train. The Thornbury branch curves to the left, while to the right of the train is Yate Main Line Junction signal box, with cattle pens and a yard crane further right.

Paul Strong

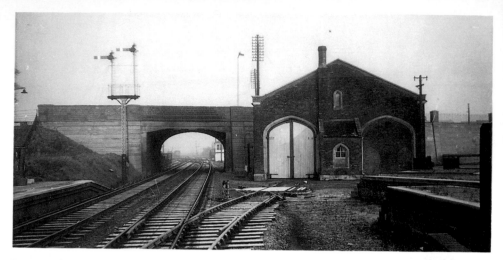

Yate goods shed after most of the track had been lifted. Notice the wagon turntable, and junction signal for the Thornbury branch; 18th February, 1961.   *D. Payne*

The plaque commemorating the celebration opening, with incorrect spelling.   *Author*

After the re-opening of Yate station on 15th May, 1989, 'Sprinter' number 150.247 arrives working the first public service train, the 6.52 am Gloucester–Temple Meads.   *Author*

YATE STATION

RE-OPENED MAY 11 1989

BY

COUNCILLOR WARREN FOSTER

CHAIRMAN AVON COUNTY COUNCIL

using the Gloucester avoiding line whilst the former called at Gloucester Eastgate.

Yate (119 miles 65 chains) and the stations northwards to Gloucester were of Brunel design and either by him, or a member of his staff. Yate itself was similar to Pangbourne and Twyford on the GWR. A pleasing design of brick, relieved with stone, the main offices were situated on the down platform, while opposite was a delightful waiting shelter in pavilion style. Both buildings had flat canopies for protecting passengers from the weather. As the awnings had no slope to enable rain water to drain off, they were weather-proofed with a sheet of lead fixed to the canopy with flat-sided, round topped battens over which the lead was rolled. This resulted in a decorative, shining ribbed surface. The main building had Tudor-style chimneys, doors and windows with a steep-gabled roof. The platforms, and those of the other stations as far as Stonehouse, were extended by Samuel Robertson in 1865 at a cost of £425 exclusive of earthworks. Mail bag apparatus was installed in 1898. The station closed to passengers in 1966.

The stone station house, and the brick goods shed, relieved with Bath stone, are still standing, the latter situated in a very cramped position between the down platform and a road overbridge. To make utmost use of the space, short sidings radiated from a wagon turntable which had flush timber decking, though the surrounding ground was not made up to this level. The main line was protected by a trap point. Most of the other B&GR stations had a similar layout.

Since the station closed, Yate has developed as a new town and its increased population called for it to be re-opened. The platforms of pink interlocking bricks are new: the down platform to the north of the overbridge and the up platform to the south. Avon County Council footed the bill for £140,000. The plastic seats in the shelters are weighted so that they automatically return to a vertical position when people get up. Both platforms have adjacent car parks. The station was officially re-opened by Councillor Warren Fowler on 11th May, 1989, but unfortunately BR made a printing error and the first plaque showed his name as 'Foster'. Public opening was on 15th May, the first train leaving at 7.17 am to Bristol. There was a Monday to Friday service of seven trains to, and six from, Bristol, the Saturday timetable offering six each way. A feeder bus from Chipping Sodbury and North Yate met almost every arrival and departure. The forecast of station usage was 150–340 journeys per day and a survey in November 1989 showed just under 300 daily. From June 1990 the service increased to nine trains to, and seven from, Bristol, the Saturday service being augmented to seven trains. At the same time the feeder bus service was extended to Hawkesbury Upton and Horton. In 1991 a ramp for the disabled was built for £70,000, the cost being shared by Avon County Council and BR. The platforms are to be extended at a cost of £125,000 to take a 4-car train.

North of the station, in 1916–7, No. 3 (Western) Aircraft Repair Depot was established. Additional traffic required the signal box to be extended in February 1919 by 12 levers, to 40 levers, three of which were spare, while in addition a ground stage was installed with six levers electrically locked and

The south and north mouths of Wickwar Tunnel, *c.*1900. *W.H. Short*

No. 3444, 0−6−0 on a freight train just leaving Wickwar Tunnel. *Lens of Sutton*

A rare rear-view of Wickwar station, showing its cramped position between road and railway, c.1963. *D. Payne*

Staff on the down platform at Wickwar, c.1905. *Author's Collection*

released from the signal box. Abandoned after World War I, George Parnall & Company took over the factory buildings in 1925. Ten years later a new undertaking was set up, Parnall Aircraft Limited, which built Fraser-Nash aircraft gun-turrets. In addition to this work, the firm also became the largest sub-contractor for Spitfire components in the country.

About a mile before Wickwar tunnel, there was a descent of 1 in 281 which continued to a point a mile beyond Charfield. This 5½ mile gradient was called Wickwar Bank.

Leading to Wickwar tunnel was a 76 ft deep cutting from which 98,000 cu. yds of mountain limestone were laboriously excavated. Edward Gale undertook this task for £5,000. A bridge over the cutting carried a stream in a trough and boards laid transversely over it provided a footwalk. This was done in 1846 after someone suggested that it would be an ideal way to restore the footpath.

In June 1840 tenders were accepted from John Strong and William Smith for two trial shafts to be sunk for the tunnel at Wickwar. They were to be 25 ft deep and 4 ft 6 in. square (or round). They were paid 20 shillings a fathom for excavating earth, but for cutting through rock, not less than 12 in. thick, 60 shillings a fathom. This estimate included keeping back water up to 100 galls per hour when a fair allowance for any extra quantity was made. These two contractors, unable to write, marked the contract with a cross.

Wickwar tunnel, 1,400 yds in length, has seven air shafts, mostly bored through mountain limestone, which was later sold for burning in a kiln. The B&GR judged that only about one-third needed a brick lining. Brunel estimated the cost of the tunnel to be £51,000 and Jonathan W. Nowell's contract for £43,994 was accepted. Nowell started work in April 1841, the 1841 census revealing that 98 workers were employed on the tunnel contract. A year later he had excavated nearly a third when wet weather caused difficulties and he became behind schedule with his work. This caused him to sink three extra shafts to regain lost time, but by September he was almost up to schedule, 825 yds being excavated and 675 totally complete. In March 1843 Brunel reported that 1,230 yds were complete and that the tunnel would be ready for permanent way by the end of the summer.

About four-ninths of the length towards the south end of the tunnel were excavated in mountain limestone of such sound quality that it was considered unnecessary to line it, all the joints and fissures being close. The northern part of the tunnel was through pennant stone, with sandstone in the centre of the tunnel and this half of the tunnel was lined or reveted with masonry or brickwork, even where it was cut through very hard sandstone, as fissures were more than 3 in. in width. The side walls of the tunnel were 18 in. thick and the arch varied from two bricks (18 in.) to two and a half bricks and even three bricks in thickness, according to the nature of the rock or shale. While the tunnel was being cut a barrel of gunpowder was placed in a blacksmith's workshop at the foot of a shaft – the results proved dire. Pool House, Wickwar, a Tudor manor, once had a lake. During the tunnel's construction, the lake was drained and a decorative tower built around the ventilating shaft which had to be sunk on the property.

Wickwar station, (115 miles 8 chains) beyond the north portal of the tunnel, had a low brick building squeezed between the platform edge and

Station master and staff on the up platform at Charfield, c.1905. A poster on the M&SWJR's bill board reads: 'Shortest & Cheapest Route to the South Coast'.

P. Strong Collection

Charfield, looking in the up direction on 11th May, 1961. Class '3F' 0−6−0 No. 43507 stands in the down loop beyond the overbridge. *Author*

The up and down loops north of Charfield station. BR Standard class '5' No. 73031 heads the 7.35 am Nottingham−Temple Meads, while class '3F' 0−6−0 No. 43507 stands in the loop beside the water column on 11th May, 1961. *Author*

Class '3F' 0−6−0 No. 43507 has drawn forward on to the main line and is passing Charfield goods shed and the bridge where the 1928 accident occurred. A van stands outside the cattle feed store: 11th May, 1961. *Author*

No. 4272 on a southbound 'local' photographed at Berkeley Road Junction on 5th July, 1947.   *H.C. Casserley*

Berkeley Road Junction on 9th July, 1959 with No. 41123 on a southbound local service.   *H.C. Casserley*

Berkeley Road, looking in the up direction, 11th May, 1961.   *Author*

Berkeley Road nameboard, 1964. 'Lydney' has been covered as the Severn Bridge was destroyed in 1960 curtailing the passenger service.
D. Payne

BR Standard class '5' 4−6−0 No. 73021 enters Berkeley Road with an up stopping passenger train on 27th June, 1964. This illustration, looking in the down direction, shows the shortened down platform.   *W. Potter*

the road below. Unlike most of the other stations, there was no canopy. A simple wooden hut did duty as a waiting shelter on the up platform. On 1st July, 1889 the words 'for Wootton-under-Edge' were added to the name-boards. On 31st December, 1900 unusually heavy rain flooded the station, sidings and tunnel. The nearby cider factory had the delightful custom of leaving a sample bucketful of their product for the crew of the daily pick-up freight! Wickwar signal box is now preserved by the Forest of Dean Railway Society.

Charfield, 113 miles 15 chains, had a more substantial building than Wickwar. Pressure is being applied locally for the station to be re-opened, together with those at Coaley and Stonehouse. In 1991 Gloucestershire County Council voted to contribute £140,000 for the construction of a new park and ride station at Charfield. It was estimated that it would generate 1,500 trips per week, 86 per cent of which would be transferred from road use, 73 per cent travelling towards Bristol and 27 per cent towards Gloucester.

Still extant north of the station site are up and down loops which, until converted in March/April 1942, had been up and down lie-bys. Beyond, a heavy embankment of 300,000 cu. yds crosses a valley and when making it, extra earth had to be dug out of the cutting to the north.

Between 1st March, 1908 and 24th March, 1963, Berkeley Loop South Junction signal box (109 miles 12 chains) gave access to the Sharpness branch.

South of Berkeley Road station is an extremely oblique over bridge, one of two in the vicinity, the other bridge being two miles north. One is 48 degrees and the other 53 degrees off the square. Both are of brick, and in the arch of the first, which was set in Roman cement, hoop iron was introduced in the manner successfully employed by Sir Marc Isambard Brunel.

Berkeley Road, (108 miles), named 'Dursley & Berkeley' until 1st June, 1845, had four platforms: two serving the main line and two the Sharpness branch. A footbridge was added in 1883, its landing supported by cast iron classical columns.

In February 1849 the inhabitants of Dursley, Uley and Coaley memorialised for a station at Cam Bridge, but the Midland declined to build one saying it was only 2¼ miles to Berkeley Road or Frocester. A station came into use on 18th September, 1856 with the opening of the Dursley & Midland Junction Railway. Dursley Junction, (105 miles, 47 chains), was renamed Coaley on 1st October, 1870. At Coaley today, a disused stone siding faces down trains. In the 1970s it was said that there was stone at Coaley and coal at Stonehouse!

Frocester station (103 miles 40 chains) had a wonderful approach by road through an avenue of beeches. The building was of stone instead of brick like the other stations described so far. The goods shed too was of stone and looked like a medieval barn. North of the station, a line brought into use on 20th May, 1915 led to Frampton Ballast Pit about four miles distant, a branch also serving a wharf at Splatt on the Gloucester & Berkeley Canal. Gravel trains to Portbury, near Portishead, where a shipyard was under

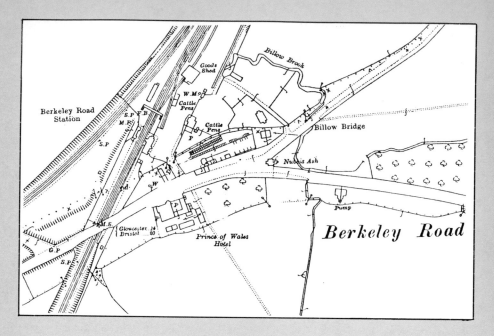

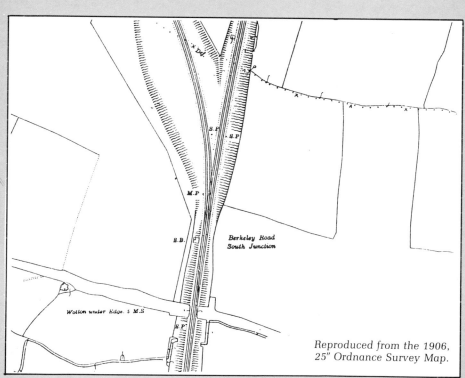

Reproduced from the 1906,
25" Ordnance Survey Map.

COALEY. M.R.

A fine view of Coaley station, station gardens and staff, all 'spick and span'. The branch train stands on the left waiting for its run to Dunsley station whilst several ladies await the mainline service. *Lens of Sutton*

A view in 1955, on a cold day in December at Coaley Junction with No. 41720 on the Dunsley Branch service and No. 45626 on a Bristol express. *Lens of Sutton*

Looking towards Bristol (from a Birmingham train) at Coaley Junction in July 1956 with the Dunsley branch single coach waiting in the branch platform. *H.C. Casserley*

Site of Coaley passenger station, now part of a stone plant; view taken on 11th May, 1991 from the cab of a down HST – which explains the windscreen wiper in the bottom right hand corner. The stone siding was, by then, out of use. *Author*

Frocester signal box pictured in 1906, with John Earl, station master, outside and signalman Isaac Plowright, inside. *Author's Collection*

Frocester, looking in the up direction, 11th May, 1961. *Author*

Frocester photographed on 27th June, 1962, looking in the down direction. The goods shed can be seen, *left*, and the gradient post indicates 1 in 366 rising/level. Notice the turntable giving access to the dock and shed. *W. Potter*

Stonehouse goods yard; main lines right; Nailsworth and Stroud branch left. *Circa* 1912. *Author's Collection.*

construction, were hauled throughout by MR engines, this particular service starting on 5th August, 1918.

Between Frocester and Stonehouse was the heaviest embankment on the line, stretching for 2¼ miles.

In the centre of the embankment near Beard's Mill, was a timber viaduct consisting of ten bays of 50 ft span, and two bays of 20 ft span, one at each end of the former, but the smaller bays were almost entirely buried in the slopes of the embankment. Two bays were over the mill dam and stream and its height from the lowest part of the surface of the ground was about 43 ft. The piers of the viaduct consisted of a framework of timber of two transverse sills, 3 ft apart at the bottom, bearing six pairs of posts, which met at the top and were crowned by six transverse double caps, each formed of two pieces of timber bolted together side by side, on which six strong longitudinal trusses were placed over the heads of the posts. The framework of every pier was supported by six pairs of the posts. The framework of every pier was supported by six pairs of piles, 13–14 in. square, driven into the ground 3 ft apart as seen in longitudinal elevation and under the rails and parapets. The principal trusses, 50 ft span, had longitudinal beams of whole timbers resting on double caps over the heads of the posts, connected with an upper course of beams of the same dimension at distances of 5½ ft by a framework of queenpost form. The uprights were 10 in. square, but the struts oblique, as well as the longitudinal pieces over the lower course of beams over the centre of each bay which were 12 in. square. All the joints of the trusses, as well as those at the head and foot of each of the posts, were secured by cast iron shoes, in addition to as many wrought iron straps, nuts and bolts as were necessary to consolidate the woodwork.

This timber viaduct was replaced by one in steel, while more recently it was rebuilt yet again, this time in steel and concrete using the brick piers from last century's rebuild. In August 1914 there was a big earth slip at the north end of the viaduct leaving sleepers hanging in mid-air. Until repairs could be effected, single line working was put into operation.

Immediately north of the viaduct a timber bridge of 30 ft span crossed the Stroudwater Canal. During construction, a penalty clause stated that for every 24 hours the canal was obstructed by the railway contractors, £50 had to be paid to the canal company. North-east of this bridge is 'The Ocean', a winding hole enlarged to act as a wharf for handling railway building materials when the B&GR was under construction.

Stonehouse, (101 miles 59 chains), had the appendage 'Bristol Road' added on 17th September, 1951 to distinguish it from the former Cheltenham & Great Western Union Railway station ½ mile distant. The Stroud and Nailsworth branch platform was separate from those serving the main line and to reach it passengers had to cross the station driveway.

The goods yard became Stonehouse Coal Concentration Depot on 7th October, 1966, dealing with about 15,000 tons of fuel annually, daily delivery to the yard varying from 2 to 20 wagons. A privately-owned locomotive shunted wagons to a pit where the hoppers were emptied and the coal carried by conveyer belt to various bins. When the locomotive failed, shunting was carried out by tractor. The depot closed in 1989, but at the time of writing the tracks are still in situ.

Stonehouse, seen looking in the up direction, *c.*1905; the station master's house is on the right. The large nameboard reads: 'Stonehouse Change for Stroud and the Nailsworth Branch'.   *Author's Collection*

Stonehouse, looking 'up' on 11th May, 1961. A goods train from the Nailsworth branch is regaining the main line.   *Author*

The drive side of Stonehouse station building, 18th February, 1961.   *D. Payne*

Dougal, a 150 hp Drewry 0–4–0 (Works No. 2251 built 1947), at Stonehouse Coal Concentration Yard on 3rd August, 1981.   *Author*

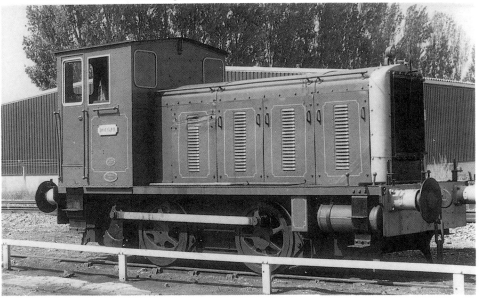

Standish Junction signal box *c.*1964, with ex-GWR tracks in the foreground and ex-LMS tracks beyond. *D. Payne*

Signalman Cyril Minnet in Standish Junction box in the 1950s. *Author's Collection*

A 'Hall' with an unidentified Saturdays-only train transferring from Midland to Western metals at Standish Junction, 20th July, 1963. *Hugh Ballantyne*

Haresfield *c.*1900 showing timber-built up platform. *Author's Collection*

Haresfield *c.*1910: the timber up platform has been replaced by one in brick. A grounded brake-third coach body acts as a store. About a dozen milk churns stand at the foot of the platform ramp. *Author's Collection*

The Cheltenham & Great Western Union Railway from Swindon joins at Standish, (100 miles 6 chains), the junction allowing the use of either MR or GWR track to and from Gloucester at one time, four lines running parallel to Tuffley. The line was reduced to double track from 7th/8th September, 1968. Unofficial racing took place between MR/LMS trains and those of the GWR. In the 1930s for example, the 'Cheltenham Spa Express' and the 'Devonian' raced each other from Tuffley to Standish, Compounds going fast and often beating the 'Castle', though the GWR often got its own back when the tank engine hauling the Chalford auto beat an LMS express.

Haresfield station, (98 miles 59 chains), with its timber-built office, opened on 29th May, 1854, the platforms only serving the Midland line. Both platforms were originally timber, but that on the up side was subsequently rebuilt in brick. The down platform was unusually narrow and squeezed between MR and GWR track, another rare feature being that it had no waiting shelter. This was of no great importance, as it was mainly used by passengers de-training after travelling from Gloucester. A further unusual feature was that it had no sidings, a fact of which not everyone was aware. A controller once told a driver to drop off there a cattle truck containing a ram.

In the early 1960s, a large hump marshalling yard to sort inter-regional traffic to and from the LMS, ER and NER, was planned to be laid at Brook-thorpe, but Beeching's closure of most local goods stations reduced the need for such shunting facilities and the plan was abandoned on 21st August, 1964. The environment would have been protected by planting trees to screen the yard, particularly the tall lighting towers.

A munitions factory was built at Quedgeley, (96 miles 54 chains), during World War I and some three miles of sidings laid. About 5,000 workers were brought from the surrounding districts by MR trains, seven days a week. The special workers' platform opened on 13th December, 1915 and closed in 1925. During World War II this factory site was brought into use as Quedgeley Depot for RAF Stores, the sidings being opened on 9th April, 1939 and since closed. Until about 1989 the Dowmac Concrete Sleeper Depot was at the south end of the Quedgeley loop.

Today, signal G121 at the north end of Quedgeley loop is unusual as it is only lit when a train is actually in the loop. If continuously lit, it would show red most of the time and could easily be thought to refer to the main line which is on a curve at this point.

At Gloucester, the line from Millstream Junction to Tramway Junction was built by the B&GR on GWR land at GWR expense to a site on Birmingham & Gloucester land by the present Gloucester station. Speed at Millstream Junction was restricted to 10 mph, and 3 mph at Tramway Junction.

The B&GR station at Gloucester had three roads: arrival, departure and central, all three connected at the last end by turntables. Working MR passenger trains in and out of a terminal station with the consequent need for reversal was time consuming and expensive, so on 12th April, 1896 a through station was opened, (93 miles 13 chains). A new line to this station from the south bore away from the parallel GWR track at Tuffley Junction, 94 miles 66 chains.

Naas Crossing box and gatekeeper's cottage, 24th February, 1967.   *D. Payne*

A 2−4−0 passing Tuffley with a Down express, *c.*1910.   *P. Strong Collection*

The buildings were in the domestic revival style of architecture, lavishly endowed with pedimented ballustrading. A typical MR ridge and furrow roof was supported by rolled steel beams on cast iron columns. The platforms were: No. 2 up through; No. 1 up bay; while on the down side was an island having platform Nos. 3 and 4.

The down side of the MR station became 'closed' for ticket purposes on 23rd November, 1914, the station being entirely 'closed' from 17th April, 1919. A consequent result of this was that the long footbridge linking the MR and GWR stations could only be used by ticket holders, this leading to criticism as inhabitants on the north side of Gloucester were unable to use the bridge to reach the MR station, or those on the south side to reach the GWR station, some citizens complaining that this was unjust treatment as the building of the bridge was a compromise when a joint station could not be opened.

'Eastgate' was added to the station's name on 17th September, 1951, while on 26th May, 1968 Eastgate and Central, (the former GWR station), were combined as 'Gloucester'. The layouts at the former Central and Eastgate stations were rationalised. At Central the former up platform was closed to the public and the former down platform extended to a length of 1977 ft, making it the longest on BR. This was partly covered by a 180 ft long steel canopy following the curve of the extension and supported by only 4 stanchions. It was built by Conder Hardware of Winchester. This long platform was No. 1. At the former Eastgate station only the island platform was retained, the line on its western face for up trains being No. 2 and the eastern for down trains, No. 3.

Eventually to make further economies, the former Eastgate station and all track from Tramway Junction to Tuffley Junction closed on 1st December, 1975, all trains now using the former GWR station.

Barton Street Junction signal box, looking in the down direction. The High Orchard branch curves to the right beyond the crossing: 9th March, 1968.   *D. Payne*

Class '4F' 0−6−0 No. 44026 at Gloucester shed on 9th August, 1956. *Hugh Ballantyne*

The High Orchard branch crossing Park End Road behind California Crossing signal box, 9th March, 1968. *D. Payne*

Class '3F' 0−6−0T No. 47417 returning from High Orchard, crosses Park End Road at California Crossing on 15th December, 1960, while a railwayman holds up a Morris 'Traveller' car. Beyond the crossing the track become double.   *S.P.J.A. Derek*

The coaster *Brier Rose* discharges cement at Victoria Dock, *c.*1930.

                                                            P. White Collection.

Class 'OF' 0−4−0T No. 41535 of 22B (Gloucester) shed, shunts at Southgate Street level crossing, the junction of the High Orchard and Docks branches on 2nd November, 1962. *Rev. Alan Newman*

Class 'OF' 0−4−0T No. 41535 at Eastgate. Notice the water column and 'devil', *left*, and the ex-GWR shed, *right*. *R.E. Toop*

Level crossings were a feature of the LMS Gloucester station, with Barton Street to the south and Tramway Crossing to the north. Both had so much road traffic that a crossing keeper had to be employed, in addition to the signalman, in order to stop traffic and close the gates. Eventually the signalman at Barton Street took control of the road traffic lights and not long afterwards, lifting barriers were installed on 3rd December, 1960. As a long up train standing at Eastgate station could foul the Barton Street crossing, when this occurred the home signal under the roof canopy was pulled off and the train drew further forward along the platform to where another water column was situated. On summer Saturdays, some through trains from the South West to the Midlands and North were routed via the ex-GWR from Standish Junction to Engine Shed Junction, Gloucester, to avoid Eastgate and its level crossings. In 1958 on peak Saturdays about 25 trains from Bristol used this diversion.

Westerleigh to Coalpit Heath

The line left the main Gloucester line at the north end of Westerleigh sidings, 7½ miles from Bristol. Beyond a level crossing over the Downend to Tormarton road, the line curved away and was between thorn hedges. In Bristol & Gloucestershire days, there was a passing loop on the curve. Then followed a straight section in a cutting about 20 ft deep. South of Boxhedge Farm, the line branched into three, making three different levels. A 6 ft tall MR mile post still marks the end of Midland territory, 1 mile from Westerleigh Junction; nearby was a weighbridge, the platform of which was fitted with three rails, for broad and narrow gauge tracks. The southern prong of the trident went to New Engine and Serridge pits (this was the original line); the centre to Church Leaze and Ram Hill pits; while the last line led to Frog Lane, Mayshill and Nibley pits. Frog Lane and Mayshill pits closed in 1949 and the branch then ceased working.

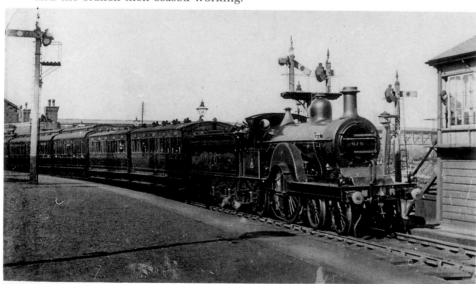

4–2–2 No. 676 at Gloucester with an up express, c.1908.   *Author's Collection*

Chapter Seven
Train Services

THE PASSENGER SERVICE

The B&GR opened with a service of six trains each way, taking about 1½ hours for the 37½ miles, calling at all, or most stations. Four up and three down trains stoped at Stonehouse, while Wickwar had the poorest service with only three trains calling in each direction. Most of the trains connected with services on the Birmingham & Gloucester Railway, and some through carriages ran to the GWR.

The down mail was the only non-stop train. It left Gloucester at 4 am and arrived at Temple Meads at 5.30. Third class coaches were only conveyed on two trains each way. Including stops, the average speed of first and second class trains was 25 mph and third class, 13 mph. Only mail trains ran on Sunday.

By July 1845 the service had increased to seven down trains, but only one conveying third class passengers. Two up trains took 2 hours, though a first-class-only express did the journey in 1 hour non-stop. Two trains each way now stopped at Mangotsfield. All down trains except the first class only, took 1½ hours. In August 1845 one train took 2 hours 5 minutes, another exactly 2 hours and a third 1 hour 53 minutes. By April 1846 the first-class-only express took 1 hour 5 minutes as it now stopped at Berkeley Road, while the rest of the trains took about 1½ hours. The seven up trains took about 2 hours except for the first class express which took only 1 hour 5 minutes. The third class train took 2¼ hours. In winter, the first-class-only train was stopped and the service reverted to only six trains each way. In March 1847 there were six stopping trains each way and three on Sundays, but by June there were seven trains again on weekdays. On 1st December, some trains were speeded up by about 5 minutes. In July 1854, the fastest narrow gauge train took 1 hour 15 minutes.

The Bristol & Birmingham Railway and MR timetables were signed by the locomotive superintendent, J.E. McConnell, or later by M. Kirtley.

The horse coach fare from Bristol to Gloucester travelling inside was 12s. and it took four hours. The rail fares were planned to be: first class 9s., second class 6s., third class 3s. 6d., but at the opening fares were reduced to: 8s., 5s. and 3s. respectively. In September 1844, inclusive tickets were issued for rail travel and admission to one performance at Gloucester Musical Festival.

When the railway opened, Robins of Wootton-under-Edge ran a bus to Charfield meeting every train. The B&GR promised to compensate him since he brought passengers to the line at a time when there was still competition from road conveyances between Bristol and Gloucester. In February 1845, Harding, the superintendent, told Robins, who ran the service at a loss, that he would be compensated for the half year to an amount not exceeding £20 on condition that no passenger, even if there was only one, should be charged more than sixpence for the trip of 2½ miles. In August 1847, a weekly payment of 17 shillings was made to Wakefield of Stroud for two seasons for working an omnibus from Stroud to Stonehouse station between 1st September and 1st March.

Gloucester (at 12.13 pm) c.1905. A 4-2-2, probably No. 94 is seen on the right, with a down express waiting at the platform. Notice the sharply curved site.

P. Strong Collection

There was a great expansion of services for the summer of 1880 when, with the co-operation of the North Eastern Railway, through passenger trains ran between Newcastle, York, Sheffield, Derby, Birmingham, Gloucester, Bristol and Bournemouth. By August 1887 the passenger service between Bristol and Gloucester had increased to 15 down and 14 up trains daily, the only non-stop up train being the Scotch Express taking 50 minutes, other expresses calling at Mangotsfield and Stonehouse. Through coaches ran to and from Bradford, Edinburgh, Glasgow, Leeds, Liverpool, Manchester, Newcastle, Sheffield and York.

By April 1910 the service had increased to 19 down and 21 up trains, the fastest taking only 45 minutes, while the 12.20 pm Bristol to York did not serve Gloucester but ran non-stop from Bristol to Cheltenham. The timetable for July 1939 showed little change in the weekday service, with 19 down and 20 up trains, the fastest taking 43 minutes. The most striking difference was on Saturdays when, due to the vast increase in the number of people taking holidays, an additional 14 down and 12 up trains were run. The timetable for the summer of 1960 showed almost exactly the same number of trains, the main difference being that the fastest down train took 46 minutes, and 49 minutes up. The frequency was little changed by the winter of 1991–2, there being 20 down and 18 up. The greatest difference is the time taken – 37 minutes which includes a stop at Bristol Parkway and also taking a route 2¾ miles longer than that of 1960.

STOPPING TRAINS

By August 1887 five down and six up services ran on weekdays, taking about 1½ hours to cover the 37 miles. By April 1910 the frequency had increased by one in each direction. The July 1922 timetable showed a reduction to six in both directions taking about 1 hr 40 mins, but by July 1938 the service had improved to seven down and eight up with the 1½ hr timing restored. Twenty years later, two less up trains were run. The last timetable before the stopping trains were withdrawn on 4th January, 1965 showed five down and four up, with a time of about 1 hr 25 mins.

Throughout the years Sunday trains remained constant at two each way, but by 1958 Haresfield, Frocester and Wickwar stations were closed on Sundays. In 1965 the only intermediate station open on Sundays was Yate, and that was only served by one up train and none in the down direction.

NAMED TRAINS

For most of the year in GWR and early BR days, the 'Devonian' was only three coaches added to a Great Western train at Temple Meads for onward working to Torbay, only in the summer did the whole train work through from Bradford to Paignton. However, by winter 1954 the complete train ran to Paignton throughout the year. The title appeared in 1927, but was withdrawn at the outbreak of war in 1939, being restored in October 1946.

The 'Cornishman' inaugurated in 1952, ran from Wolverhampton and Stratford-upon-Avon over lines of the former Great Western Railway to Cheltenham and on via Bristol to Plymouth and Cornwall. The 'Pines Express', which started in October 1910, ran from Manchester, via

DERBY, BIRMINGHAM, GLOUCESTER, BRISTOL, and WEST OF ENGLAND

Down. — **Week Days**—*Continued.*

	Down.	aft	aft	mrn	mrn	mrn	mrn	mrn	mrn	mrn	mrn	mrn	mrn	aft	aft	mrn	mrn	mrn	mrn	aft	aft
—	Gloucester .... dep.	TC Bradford and Leeds to To	on night · Friday night an Saturday morni		2 48	2 57	2 57	4 40	6 40	5 28	7 30	7 55	9 5	TC goin	9 25	10 1	..	..	..	1026	1036	..
98¼	Harestield				TC from Colne, pp. 608 & 585.	..	..	TC Newcastle to Bristol.	..	..	..	8 5	..		..	1012	..	..	..	..	..	..
101½	Stonehouse F 698					..	..		6 56	..	7 46	8 14	..		9 39	1020	..	..	..	E	1051	..
103¾	Frocester					..	..		..	..	..	8 20	..		..	1026	..	..	..	..	..	..
105¾	Coaley 685					..	..		7 5	..	7 53	8 26	..		..	1031	..	..	..	..	..	..
107¾	Berkeley Road 1084					..	..			..	7 58	8 33	..	..	..	1037	..	..	..	..	11E1	..
113	Charfield G					..	..		..	..	8 8	8 42	..	..	..	1047	..	..	..	..	..	..
115	Wickwar					..	..		..	..	8 14	8 47	..	..	..	1053	..	..	..	..	..	..
119½	Yate H 714					..	..		..	..	8 24	8 57	..	..	..	11 3	..	..	..	..	..	..
124¾	Mangotsfield 725					..	..	5 21	..	6 14	8 33	9 6	9 45	..	..	1111	..	..	..	..	1123	..
134½	725 Bath (Queen Square) .. arr.				3 52	4 5	4 5	6 27	..	6 40	9 17	9 37	1016	..	1030	12 1	..	..	..	1130	12 1	..
206¼	1076 Bournemouth West .. "				6 39	7 7	7 7	10 46	..	1046	1130	1255	1255	..	1255	4A5	..	..	..	2 3	4A5	..
126	Staple Hill				..	..	..	..	..	..	8 39	9 16	..	..	..	1117	..	..	..	..	..	..
126¾	Fish Ponds 725 ... [56, 57, 64				..	..	..	..	..	..	8 43	9 20	..		..	1120	..	..	..	..	..	..
129¾	Bristol J 14, 20, 52, 53, arr.			3 40	..	..	..	5 37	..	6 35	8 51	9 30	10 0	..	..	1128	..	..	..	..	1136	..

Gloucester .... dep.	1127	11 37		☞	..	12 5	...rough Exp., Lincoln (dep. 8 30 ... TC to Bristol, going	1224	1233	1233	1255	Except	1 3	1 13	1 21		1 27	1 31	1 41	1 59	..
Harestield	..	RC Sheffield to Gloucester.	RC Sheffield to Gloucester.		..	Saturdays only.		RC Nottingham to Bristol.	RC Derby to Bristol.	..	..	TC Bradford & Leeds to B	Express Sheffield to Bournemouth	RC Derby to Bristol.	..	TC Liverpool (L. St.) and	..	The Pines Express.	The Pines Express.	RC Nottingham to Bath	..
Stonehouse F 698	..				..					..	..				..		..				..
Frocester	..				..					..	..				..		..				..
Coaley 710	..				..					..	..				..		..				..
Berkeley Road 1084	..				..					..	..				..		..				..
Charfield G	..				..					..	..				..		..				..
Wickwar	..			aft	..					..	..				..		..				..
Yate H 714	..			1225	..					..	..				..		..				..
Mangotsfield 725	..			1233	..					..	..				..		..				..
725 Bath (Queen Square) .. arr.	..		..	1 12	..	1255				1 27	1 50		1 50		2 10		2 15	2 20	2 36	2 48	..
1076 Bournemouth West .. "	..		..	..	..	3 4				..	4 5		4 5		4 22		4 37	4 37	4 53	5 8	..
Staple Hill	..		..	1238	..	..				..	..		..	..	..		..	..	..	..	..
Fish Ponds 725 ... [56, 57, 64	..	..	..	1240	..	..				..	..		..	..	..		..	..	..	..	..
Bristol J 14, 20, 52, 53, arr.	1213	12 33	..	..	..	..		1 16	1 25	..	..		..	2 0	..		..	..	..	..	..

Gloucester .... dep.	1 55	2 5	2 35	..	2 48		3 2	3 8	3 18	3 40	..	..	4 10	4 5	..	..	4 56	5 3	5 10
Haresfield	2 6	2 16	..	..	TC Newcastle to Bristol		..	..	..	..	..	..	4 21		..	..	..	..	..
Stonehouse F 698	2 14	2 23	..	..		..	..	..	..	3 55	..	..	4 28	..	..	..	5 11	5 17	..
Frocester	2 19	2 27	..	..		..	..	..	..	..	..	..	4 33	..	..	..	..	..	..
Coaley 685	2 25	2 32	..	..		..	..	..	..	4 2	..	..	4 38	..	..	..	..	..	..
Berkeley Road 1084	2 32	2 38	..	..		..	..	..	..	4 8	..	..	4 44	..	..	..	..	..	..
Charfield G	2 43	2 47	..	..		..	..	..	..	..	..	..	4 52	..	..	..	..	..	..
Wickwar	2 49	2 52	..	..		..	..	..	..	..	..	..	4 57	..	aft	..	..	..	..
Yate H 714	2 58	3 1	..	..		..	..	..	..	..	..	..	5 6	..	5 17	..	..	..	..
Mangotsfield 725	3 6	3 9	..	..		..	..	..	..	4 30	..	..	5 20	..	5 27	..	5 40	5 49	6 5
725 Bath (Queen Square) .. arr.	3 44	3 44	..	..		..	..	3 56	..	4o58	..	..	6 15	4 56	6 15	..	6 15	6 24	6 45
1076 Bournemouth West .. "	6 15	6n16	..	..		..	..	6 16	..	..	..	..	..	7 13	1018	.	1018	1018	1018
Staple Hill	3 12	3 15	..	..		..	..	..	..	..	..	..	..	..	5 32	..	..	..	..
Fish Ponds 725 ... [56, 57, 64	3 16	3 18	..	..		..	..	..	..	..	..	..	..	..	5 37	..	..	..	..
Bristol J 14, 20, 52, 53, arr.	3 24	3 26	..	..	3 32	3 35	3 46	..	4 8	4 43	..	..	5 40	..	5 45	..	5 54	6 5	6 20

Gloucester .... dep.	5 46	..	..	..	6 49	..	6 50	7 5	7 20	..	..	..	..	Teas and a	on	..	9 30	9 25	1130	..	..	..
Haresfield	5 57	..	..	..	RC Derby to Bristol	..	..	..	7 31	..	..	..	..		Mons. and also on 29th	..	9 41		..	..	..	..
Stonehouse F 698	6 5	..	..	..		..	..	..	7 38	..	..	..	..			..	9 48	..	1144	..	..	..
Frocester	6 11	..	..	..		..	..	..	7 44	..	..	..	..			..	9 53	..	..	..	..	..
Coaley 685	6 16	..	..	..		..	..	..	7 49	..	..	..	..			..	9 58	..	..	..	..	..
Berkeley Road 1084	6 23	..	..	..		..	..	..	7 56	..	..	..	..			..	10 4	..	..	..	..	..
Charfield G	6 33	..	..	..		..	..	..	8 4	..	..	..	..			..	10 13	..	..	..	..	..
Wickwar	6 38	..	..	..		..	..	..	8 9	..	..	..	..			..	10 18	..	..	..	..	..
Yate H 714	6 47	..	..	..		..	..	..	8 18	..	..	..	..			..	10 27	..	..	..	..	..
Mangotsfield 725	6 55	..	..	..	7 27	..	7 25	7 46	8 26	..	..	..	..			..	10 35	9 59	..	..	..	..
725 Bath (Queen Square) ... arr.	7 28	..	..	..	8 20	..	8 20	8 20	8 56	..	..	..	..	..		..	11S25	1038	..	..	..	..
1076 Bournemouth West .. "	..	..	..	..	..	..	..	..	..	..	..	..	..	..		..	..	..	..	..	..	..
Staple Hill	7 4	..	..	..	..	..	..	..	8 33	..	..	..	..	..	..	..	..	..	..	..	..	..
Fish Ponds 725 .... [56, 57, 64	7 8	..	..	..	..	..	..	..	8 37	..	..	..	..	..	..	..	10 42	..	..	..	..	..
Bristol J 14, 20, 52, 53, arr.	7 16	..	..	..	7 40	..	7 40	8 7	8 45	..	..	..	..	..	..	..	10 50	1011	1220	..	..	..

Sundays

				Sat																	
				aft	aft	mrn	aft	aft	mrn	mrn	mrn	aft	mrn	aft	mrn	mrn	aft	aft	aft	aft	aft
Gloucester .... dep.	..	..	..	4 50	5 28	8 55	11 16	1220	..	2 48	..	..	..	..	..	5 37	7 30	..	..	1130	..
Haresfield	..	..	..	TC Newcastle to Bristol.	..	9 6	..	..	..	..	..	..	..	..	..	..	7 41	..	..	..	..
Stonehouse F 698	..	..	..		..	9 12	..	..	..	..	..	..	..	..	..	..	7 48	..	..	1144	..
Frocester	..	..	..		..	..	..	..	..	..	..	..	..	..	..	..	..	..	..	..	..
Coaley 685	..	..	..		..	9 21	..	..	..	..	..	..	..	..	..	..	7 56	..	..	..	..
Berkeley Road 1084	..	..	..		..	9 28	..	..	..	..	..	..	..	..	..	..	8 4	..	..	..	..
Charfield G	..	..	..		..	9 37	..	..	..	..	..	..	..	..	..	..	8 13	..	..	..	..
Wickwar	..	..	..		..	9 44	..	..	..	..	..	..	..	..	..	..	8 18	..	..	..	..
Yate H 714	..	..	..		..	9 55	..	..	..	..	..	..	..	..	..	..	8 28	..	..	..	..
Mangotsfield 725	..	..	..	5 33	6 14	10 2	..	..	..	..	..	..	..	..	..	6 17	8 36	..	..	..	..
725 Bath (Queen Square) .. arr	..	..	..	..	..	1040	..	..	..	..	..	..	..	..	..	6 45	9 5	..	..	..	..
1076 Bournemouth West .. "	..	..	..	..	..	1 17	..	..	..	..	..	..	..	..	..	..	..	..	..	..	..
Staple Hill	..	..	..	..	..	10 8	..	..	..	..	..	..	..	..	..	..	8 46	..	..	..	..
Fish Ponds 725 ... [56, 57, 64	..	..	..	..	..	1012	..	..	..	..	..	..	..	..	..	..	8 49	..	..	..	..
Bristol J 14, 20, 52, 53, arr.	..	..	..	5 50	6 35	1020	12 5	1 20	..	3 40	..	..	..	..	..	6 36	8 57	..	..	1220	..

Gloucester .... dep.	..	..	..	..	4 40
Haresfield	..	..	..	..	TC Newcastle to Bristol.
Stonehouse F	..	..	..	..	
Frocester	..	..	..	..	
Coaley	..	..	..	..	
Berkeley Road	..	..	..	..	
Charfield G	..	..	..	..	
Wickwar	..	..	..	..	
Yate H	..	..	..	..	
Mangotsfield 725	..	..	..	..	5 21
725 Bath (Queen Square) .. arr.	..	..	..	..	6 27
Bournemouth West .. "	..	..	..	..	1046
Staple Hill	..	..	..	..	..
Fish Ponds 725 .... [56, 67	..	..	..	..	..
Bristol J 18, 24, 52, 53, arr.	..	..	..	..	5 37

Extracts from the July 1938 'Bradshaw' timetables.

WEST OF ENGLAND, BRISTOL, GLOUCESTER, BIRMINGHAM, and DERBY.

Miles	Up.	Week Days.																		
		mrn	mrn		aft	mrn	mrn	mrn	mrn	mrn	mrn	mrn	mrn	mrn	mrn	mrn	mrn	mrn	mrn	mrn
—	**Bristol** (Temple Meads)....dep.	1 10	..		..	2 10	..	..	..	..	6 45		..	..	..	..	..	..	7 42	8 25
3	Fish Ponds 725	..	..		..		..	..	..	..	6 57		..	..	..	..	..	..	..	8 32
3¾	Staple Hill	..	..		..		..	..	..	..	7 0		..	..	..	..	..	..	..	8 35
—	1077 Bournemouth West...dep	..	..		11d0		..	..	..	..	..		..	..	..	..	..	..	..	..
—	725 Bath (Queen Square)... "	..	..		..		..	..	..	..	6 30		..	..	..	..	..	..	7 22	..
5	Mangotsfield 725	..	..		..		..	..	..	..	7 7		..	..	..	..	..	..	7 58	8 39
10½	Yate H 714	..	..		..		..	..	..	..	7 19		..	..	..	..	..	..	..	8 49
14½	Wickwar	..	..	4 45 mrn. ... 413 and 588.	..	Saturdays only. Except 9th inst.	..	..	..	..	7 30	...e meals served ...ain to Sheffield.	..	..	..	..	..	..	..	Stop
16½	Charfield G	..	..		..		..	..	..	..	7 36		..	..	..	..	..	..	..	..
22	Berkeley Road 1084	..	..		..		..	..	..	..	7 46		..	..	..	..	..	..	8 17	..
24½	Coaley 685	..	..		..		..	..	..	..	7 54		..	..	..	..	..	..	8 22	..
26½	Frocester [698	..	..		..		..	..	..	..	8 0		..	..	..	..	..	..	..	..
28½	Stonehouse (Eastington Rd.)	1 53	..		..		..	..	..	..	8 6		..	..	..	..	..	..	..	..
31½	Haresfield [140	..	..		mrn		..	..	..	..	8 16		..	..	..	..	..	..	..	..
37	**Gloucester D** 74, 75, 128 arr.	2 7	..		2 26	2 54	..	..	..	..	8 25		..	..	..	..	..	..	8 38	..

Up.																							
	mrn	mrn	mrn	mrn	aft	mrn	mrn	aft	aft	aft	aft	mrn	mrn	mrn	mrn		mrn		mrn		mrn		aft
Bristol (Temple Meads)...dep.	..	..	9 5	9 19	..	1030	1035	..	..	..	..	..	..	1050	1120		..		..		..		..
Fish Ponds 725	..	..	..	9 30	..	..	..	..	..	..	..	..	..	11 0	..		..		..		..		..
Staple Hill	..	..	..	9 33	..	..	..	..	..	..	..	..	..	11 3	..		..		..		..		..
1077 Bournemouth West..dep.	..	..	..	..	..	..	..	..	..	..	..	..	..	..	..		9 45		10 0		10 0		..
725 Bath (Queen Square).. "	..	..	8 37	8 37	..	1020	1020	..	..	..	..	..	..	1020	..		1145		12 8		12 8		..
Mangotsfield 725			9 20	9 39	..	1045	1050	..	..	..	..			11 8									..
Yate H 714			..	9 49	..			..	..	..	..			1118									..
Wickwar	Saturdays only	Except Saturdays.	..	9 57	..	Saturdays only.	Except Saturdays	..	..	..	..	Except Saturdays	Saturdays only.	1126	Saturdays only.	...nd 700.	Saturdays only.	...radford	Saturdays only.	...ds and Bradford.	Mons. & Fris.	see pages 689, 644 & 700.	Saturdays only.
Charfield G			.	10 2	..			..	..	..	..			1131									..
Berkeley Road 1084			9 40	1015	..			..	..	..	..			1140									..
Coaley 685			..	1022	..			..	..	..	..			1145									..
Frocester [698			..	1028	..			..	..	..	..			1150									..
Stonehouse (Eastington Rd.)			9 49	1034	..			..	..	..	..			1155									..
Haresfield [140			.	1041	..			..	..	..	..			12 2									..
Gloucester D 74, 75, 128, ar			10 0	1048	..	1118	1123	.	..	..	..	..		12 9	1220				1257		1257		1 6

Up.																						
		aft		aft	mrn		mrn	mrn		aft	aft		aft	aft	aft	mrn	mrn	aft	mrn		aft	aft
Bristol (Temple Meads)....dep.		..		12 35	..		..	..	One ... onl...	1255	..		..	..	..	..	..	1 14	..		2 20	
Fish Ponds 725		..			..		..	..		..	..		..	..	..	..	..	1 24	..		..	
Staple Hill		..			..		..	..		..	..		..	..	..	..	..	1 27	..		..	
1077 Bournemouth West dep.		..			1020		1035	1035	..	..	..		..	..	..	..	..	E 1035	1140		Z 1140	
725 Bath (Queen Square) "		..			1233		1244	1244	..	..	..		1257	..	..	..	..	D 1250	2 0		2Z 0	
Mangotsfield 725							..			..	..		..	..	..			1 31			2†38	
Yate H 714							..			..	..		..	..	..			1 41			..	
Wickwar	...and 21a.	Saturdays only.	...31 & 21a.	Except Saturdays	Saturdays only.	C On Tues., Weds. and Thurs. ... 3 4 aft.	..	Saturdays only.	Great Malvern, arr. ...5 aft., see page 686.	..	..	...ges 175a and 1077.	..	..	..	Except Saturdays	Saturdays only.	1 49	Mons., Fris., and Sats.	...o Bristol to Leicester, Nottingham ... at 4 55 aft.	..	...ningham to Leicester, ...146, and 700.
Charfield G							..			..	..		..	..	..			1 54			..	
Berkeley Road 1084							..			..	..		..	..	..			2 3			..	
Coaley 685							..			1 34	..		..	..	..			2 8			..	
Frocester [698							..			..	..		..	..	..			2 13			..	
Stonehouse (Eastington Road)							..			..	..		..	..	..			2 18			..	
Haresfield [140							..			..	..		..	..	..			2 25			..	
Gloucester D 74, 75, 128. arr.		1 18		1 18	..		1 32	1 40		1 50	..		2 0	..	..			2 32	2 56		3 11	

Up.																					
	aft	aft	aft	aft	aft	aft	aft	aft	aft	aft	aft	aft	aft	aft	aft	aft	aft	aft	aft	aft	aft
Bristol (Temple Meads).....dep.	2 45	2 52	3 25	..	..	..	2E52	..	4 20	4 20	5 0	5 0	..	..	5 11	..	5 40	..	..	..	5E11
Fish Ponds 725		3 2	.	..	..	..	3E2	..	..	..	..	..	..	..	5 21	..	..	..	..	..	5E21
Staple Hill		..	..	..	..	..	3E5	..	..	..	..	..	..	..	5 25	..	..	..	..	..	5E25
1077 Bournemouth West....dep.		1140	..	..	..	..	E 1140	1 50	1 50	..	..	..	..	2 45	.	..	..	..	..	..	..
725 Bath (Queen Square).... "		2 27	..	..	..	..	2E10	4 0	4 6	4 6	..	..	..	5 9	4 50	..	4 50	..	..	..	4E50
Mangotsfield 725		3 7		..	..	..	3E10		4 37	4 39			..		5 30	..	5 58	..	..	..	5E30
Yate H 714		3 17		..	..	..	3E20			..			..		5 40	..		..	..	..	5E40
Wickwar	Saturdays only.	..	Saturdays only.	..	..	..	3E28	Saturdays only.	Sats. only.	..	Except Saturdays.	Saturdays only	..	Saturdays only.	5 48	..	Sats. only.	..	..	..	5E48
Charfield G		3 27		..	..	..	3E33			..			..		5 53	..		..	..	..	5E53
Berkeley Road 1084		3 36		..	..	..	3E42			..			..		6 2	..		..	..	..	6E2
Coaley 685		3 41		..	..	..	3E48			..			..		6 10	..		..	..	..	6E10
Frocester [698		..		..	..	..	3E54			..			..		6 16	..		..	..	..	6E16
Stonehouse (Eastington Road) F		3 49		..	..	..	4E0		5 4	5 9			..		6 21	..	6 29	..	..	..	6E21
Haresfield [140		..		..	..	..	4E7		..	5 17			..		6 28	..	..	..	..	..	6E28
Gloucester D 74, 75, 128, arr.	3 30	4 0	4 13	..	..	..	4E15	4 52	5 15	5 24	5 43	5 43	..	6 4	6 35	..	6 43	..	..	..	6E35

Up.	Week Days—*Continued*													Sundays.							Sat.
	aft	aft		aft		aft	aft	aft	aft	aft	aft	aft		mrn	mrn	mrn	mrn	mrn	mrn	mrn	mrn
Bristol (Temple Meads).....dep.	6 20	6 37		7 20		..	..	8*0	..	9 25	1115	1145	..	..	1 10	..	..	..	..	.	8 0
Fish Ponds 725	6 32	..		..		..	..	..	..	9 35	1126	..	..	..	..	..	..	..	..	..	8 12
Staple Hill	6 35	..		..		..	..	..	..	9 38	..	..	..	..	..	..	..	..	..	..	8 16
1077 Bournemouth West....dep.	E	1250		3 45	5 0	..	..	..	..	..	7 38		..	..	..	..	..	..	..	..	..
725 Bath (Queen Square).... "	6 12	6 12		7 8	7 35	..	..	7 45	..	7 45	1030		..	..	..	..	..	..	..	..	..
Mangotsfield 725	6 42	6 55		7 40	..	..	..	8 23		9 42	1131		..	..	..	..	..	..	..	..	8 24
Yate H 714	6 55	7 5		..	..	..	..	8 33		9 52	1142		..	..	..	..	..	..	..	..	8 34
Wickwar	Stop	7 13	(via Crewe), except on Sats.	..	Satur... onl...	..	..	..	Saturdays only.	10 0	1151	Except Saturdays.	..	..	..	..	..	..	..	..	8 43
Charfield G		7 18		..	..	..	..	..		10 5	1156		..	..	..	..	..	..	..	..	8 49
Berkeley Road 1084	..	7 29		..	..	..	..	..		1014	12 5		..	..	..	..	..	..	..	..	9 3
Coaley 685	..	7 35		..	..	..	..	..		1019	1211		..	..	..	..	..	..	..	..	9 9
Frocester [698	aft	..		..	..	..	..	..		..	..		..	..	..	..	..	..	..	..	..
Stonehouse (Eastington Road)	7 30	7 45		..	..	..	..	..		1026	1218	..	..	..	1 53	..	..	..	..	..	9 19
Haresfield [140	..	7S52		..	..	..	..	..		..	..	..	..	..	..	..	..	..	..	..	9 27
Gloucester D 74, 75, 128, arr.	7 45	8 0		8 21	8 40	..	..	9 3		1038	1233	1245	..	..	2 7	..	..	..	..	..	9 35

	mrn	mrn	aft	aft	aft	aft	aft	aft	aft	aft	aft		aft	aft	aft
Bristol (Temple Meads).....dep.	8 50	9 35	.	2 0	..	3 20	..	..	..	5 10	6 45		7 20	..	8 35
Fish Ponds 725	9 1	9 47	..	..	..	..	..	..	..	5 20	6 55		..	..	8 48
Staple Hill	..	9 51	..	..	..	..	..	..	..	5 23	..		..	..	..
Bournemouth West....dep.	..	..	..	..	..	..	..	..	..	..	..		4 42	..	..
725 Bath (Queen Square).... "	8 30	9 30	..	..	..	..	..	..	..	..	5 45		7 0	..	..
Mangotsfield 725	9 10	9 56	..	..	..	..	..	..	..	5 28	7 4		7 40	..	..
Yate H	..	10 7	..	..	..	..	..	..	..	5 38	..		..	..	..
Wickwar	..	..	..	..	..	..	..	..	..	5 47	..	...ningham (via Crewe).	..	..	..
Charfield G	9 28	1018	..	..	..	..	..	..	..	5 53	7 22		..	..	..
Berkeley Road	9 37	..	..	..	..	..	..	..	..	6 2	7 31		..	..	..
Coaley	..	..	..	..	..	..	..	..	..	6 7	7 36		..	..	..
Frocester	..	..	..	..	..	..	..	..	..	..	..		..	..	..
Stonehouse (Eastington Road)	..	1033	..	..	..	..	..	..	..	6 14	7 43		..	..	..
Haresfield	..	..	..	..	..	..	..	..	..	6 22	7 51		..	..	..
Gloucester D 74, 75, 128 arr.	9 58	1046	..	2 48	..	4 2	..	..	..	6 29	7 58		8 21	..	9 33

BR Standard class '5' 4−6−0 No. 73069 passes Berkeley Road with the down 'Devonian', on 14th June, 1958.   *R.E. Toop*

A 3-car dmu passes Mangotsfield North Junction with the 11.25 am Bristol−Worcester on 19th April, 1969. The Bath branch, *left*, has been singled and the main line is protected by a GWR-pattern signal.   *Hugh Ballantyne*

Birmingham to Bournemouth, using the line as far as Mangotsfield North Junction where it diverged to Bath.

The winter 1991–2 timetable shows quite a clutch of named HST trains: 'The Devon Scot' Aberdeen–Plymouth; 'The Cornish Scot' Glasgow–Penzance; 'The Cornishman' Dundee–Penzance; 'The Armada' Leeds–Plymouth; and 'The Devonian' Leeds–Paignton.

SPECIAL TRAINS AND GENERAL POST OFFICE SERVICES

Some of the early excursion trains were of gargantuan proportions. In September 1846, 4,000 Sunday school children and 500 teachers and friends travelled from Bristol to Gloucester in two trains of 29 coaches each. Their return was even more spectacular for this was in ' . . . one enormous train consisting of 58 carriages drawn and propelled by seven engines, four of which went the whole distance' (Gloucester Journal, 12th September, 1846). The three bankers probably assisted to Standish Junction. In June 1851, for their annual treat, the Great Western Cotton Works, Bristol gave their employees an outing to Cheltenham, the 1,700 passengers in 55 coaches being hauled by three engines.

To speed mail services, a sorting van was running with the Bristol–Newcastle Mail by March 1855 and lineside apparatus had been installed at Stonehouse and Charfield. By 1898 mail exchange apparatus was also in use at Fishponds, Mangotsfield, Yate, Wickwar, Charfield, Berkeley Road and Stonehouse. The vehicles, jointly owned by the MR and NER, were lettered M&NEJPS*. As the exchange apparatus was only on one side of the vehicles, before being returned to Newcastle they had to be turned on the triangle at Mangotsfield.

The serious accident at Charfield in 1928 (described later) involved the South Mail. During World War II the TPO was suspended from 21st September, 1939 until 6th May, 1946.

FREIGHT AND MINERAL TRAFFIC

In 1844, £15,000 was granted by the Directors to develop coal and lime traffic. This sum was to be issued as loan notes to parties which had ample security. Goods service started on 1st September, 1844 and coal traffic a week later, but the line and arrangements were so imperfect that it curbed business. In October the Directors wrote to the Great Western to say that there was insufficient room for goods at Bristol. 'The present trade which is not one-third of what may be anticipated, requires six trucks throughout the day along the outward platform. As the outward platform only holds 11 trucks including the traversing frame, and the Great Western take up nine, the Bristol & Gloucester only have room for two or at the most, three trucks on the platform.' Wagons were kept waiting for hours. The platform was narrow and goods were frequently mis-sorted. Both companies shared a common lift. After the Great Western goods at 7.30 pm, there was a B&GR goods at 4.30 am and another GWR goods at 5.30 am. The congestion was such that there was no room to unload these three trains.

The GWR had six goods trains using the station. The B&GR goods had to leave before the up Great Western goods came in at 7.30 pm, entailing the

* Midland & North Eastern Joint Postal Stock.

B&GR closing its doors at 5 pm and even then, 2½ hours was insufficient to complete loading and invoicing. Competing road vans travelling to Gloucester accepted goods until 4 pm and arrived in Gloucester for next morning's delivery, and thus the railway had little advantage over them. The GWR did not close until 8 pm and more goods were sent in from 5 to 8 pm than during the rest of the day.

The B&GR anticipated difficulties when trains of 30 of its loaded wagons came in. In May 1845 the Great Western promised to build a larger goods shed, after J.D. Payne, B&GR goods manager, made further complaints. New goods offices were opened by the B&GR in December 1846.

Goods traffic at Gloucester was dealt with in a joint shed built by the Bristol and Birmingham companies and enlarged in June 1849.

Charges for carrying coal from 3 to 10 miles were 2½d. per ton/mile, with wharfage and weighing dues 1d. ton and shipping dues 1d. ton. This compared with freight by water from Gloucester to Bristol of 8s. 6d. ton (this works out to approximately 2½d. ton/mile in a straight line) taking five days; freight by road Gloucester to Bristol, 8⅔d. ton/mile taking 24 hours. In August 10d. a ton was quoted for carrying bricks from Shortwood to Bristol. In January 1846 the GPO offer of 8d. per mile for night mail from Bristol to Gloucester, and day mail from Bristol to Birmingham was approved.

A train of more than 12 wagons could be divided to get it up the incline to Staple Hill. At the head of the incline a banking engine had to return on the down line, provided no train was due for half an hour. If it was, the banker had to wait and then descend after it. All down trains arriving at the 3½ mile post at the head of the 1 in 72 were required to reduce speed to 8 mph, and the fireman had to make the brake touch the wheel to keep the speed down to 10 mph, while the driver stood ready to reverse the engine if the need should arise. Before entering Bristol station the engine was required to be completely stopped.

'Patriot' class 4–6–0 No. 45504 *Royal Signals* leaves a Newcastle-bound train, having piloted 'Jubilee' class 4–6–0 No. 45685 *Barfleur* from Temple Meads, 9th September, 1960.
R.E. Toop

Chapter Eight

Locomotives

At first the B&GR intended the Great Western to work the line, but negotiations fell through as the companies could not agree on terms. The B&GR decided to buy its own engines, and Brunel drew out a specification for six passenger and three goods tender engines, and sent copies to eight locomotive builders in August 1843 and also advertised in the railway journals.

However, on 2nd October, 1843 the Directors entered into a contract with Stothert, Slaughter & Co. to furnish the entire plant and work the line for 10 years on satisfactory terms. Thus outlay for repairing shops and engine houses was avoided.

The locomotives had characteristic Bury inside frames and D-shaped fireboxes with a domed brass top. As the drawings were initialled 'B.C. & K. and S.S.Co' it is likely that they were built by Bury, Curtis & Kennedy and the parts shipped to Bristol where they were re-assembled by Stothert, Slaughter & Co. The 0−6−0s were probably built by the Vulcan Foundry as their Rotation Numbers 163 and 164 of 1842 show the supply of two broad gauge 0−6−0s with 5 ft diameter wheels and 16 in. by 20 in. cylinders to the 'contractors of the Birmingham & Gloucester Railway' − certainly an erroneous entry as the Birmingham & Gloucester was a standard gauge line. The order should have read 'Bristol & Gloucester'.

Locomotive running costs worked out at 11½d. a mile − the same as the GWR − but they ran heavier trains. Stothert, Slaughter housed the 11 engines which were to be used, in the Great Western carriage sheds until the line was ready. The Midland purchased these 11 engines used on the B&GR from Stothert's in July 1845.

When McConnell gave evidence before the Gauge Commission, he said that one of Slaughter's largest goods engines, with a pilot engine up the incline to Staple Hill, hauled a gross load of 235 tons and covered the 37½ miles to Gloucester in 4 hours 13 minutes including four stops. At Gloucester the freight was transhipped into narrow gauge wagons and they left with a load of 254 tons. McConnell rode on the engine and the 51 miles from Gloucester to Camp Hill station, Birmingham, was covered in 3 hours 55 minutes with six stops and banking up the Lickey Incline. This gave speeds of 8¾ mph on the broad gauge and 13 mph on the narrow gauge. This does not prove anything conclusive, except that it shows McConnell made a good run on the narrow gauge.

In August 1846, tenders were to be obtained for two broad gauge tender locomotives. Stothert, Slaughter, priced them at £2,500 each and one additional coal tender at £500. The Board accepted this, but a few days later, Stothert, Slaughter said they were unable to comply. McConnell could not get any tenders from elsewhere, and Barlow was requested to arrange for the immediate erection of a workshop at Gloucester and for a broad gauge engine to be built there. However, before concrete steps were taken, Sharp Bros offered to build a broad gauge engine for £3,000 and deliver in nine months.

McConnell was appointed to the London & North Western Railway early in 1847 and Matthew Kirtley offered to take over the locomotive superintendency immediately, so that McConnell could be released as soon as possible. The Directors' minutes of 27th February, 1847 state: 'Resolved that intimation be given to Mr McConnell that Mr Kirtley is now in charge of the Locomotive Department and that the Secretary do assure Mr McConnell that the Directors are much gratified that his efficiency on the Bristol & Birmingham Railway has ended in promotion to his present important position.'

In April, Kirtley countermanded the order for the broad gauge engine and instead ordered four narrow gauge engines at £2,130 each and four tenders at £480. Kirtley instructed Sharp Bros to build them convertible (they were the first convertible engines ever to be built). They were narrow gauge locomotives with long axles, and at first, while being used on the broad gauge, the wheels were outside the axleboxes. Numbered 66–69, they had cylinders 16 in. by 20 in. and 6 ft 6 in. driving wheels. When the narrow gauge was ready (opened 29th May, 1854), they had the axles shortened and the wheels placed inside the double frame, and were back on the road within 24 hours.

Most of the original B&GR engines were sold by Midland, and saw a second lifetime on the broad gauge North Devon Railway, working first for the lessee Thomas Brassey,and then for the LSWR when they took over.

B&GR locomotives had two whistles: a small warning one in front of the firebox, and the 'guard's whistle' with a deeper tone on the right hand side, blown when the driver required additional braking power. To signal to the guard to release the brakes, the deep tone and the small whistle were alternated twice. If banking assistance was required, a driver gave two long beats on the small whistle if it was dark or merely a hand signal in the daylight hours and the banker would come out of its siding and gently catch up the moving train.

MR 4–4–0 No. 413 and a 2–4–0 at Temple Meads with a down stopping train, c.1920.   *W. Vaughan-Jenkins*

LOCOMOTIVES

Name	B&GR No.	MR No.	Dia. of driving wheels	Weight (tons)	Cylinders (inside)	Wheel	Builder
Tugwell	1	268 368 468	5'	17½	15" × 18"	2–4–0	Bury, Curtis & Kennedy (?)
Industry	2	269 369 469	5'	17½	15" × 18"	2–4–0	,,
Pilot	3	270	5'	17½	15" × 18"	2–4–0	,,
Bristol	4	260 360 460	6' 6"	18	15" × 21"	2–2–2	Bury, Curtis & Kennedy
Gloucester	5	261 361 461	6' 6"	18	15" × 21"	2–2–2	,,
Berkeley	6	262 362 462	6' 6"	18	15" × 21"	2–2–2	,,
Wickwar	7	263 363	6' 6"	18	15" × 21"	2–2–2	,,
Cheltenham	8	264 364 464	6' 6"	18	15" × 21"	2–2–2	,,
Stroud	9	265 365 465	6' 6"	18	15" × 21"	2–2–2	,,
Dreadnought	10	266 366 466	5'	26	16" × 21"	0–6–0	Vulcan Foundry
Defiance	11	267 367 467	5'	26	16" × 21"	0–6–0	,,

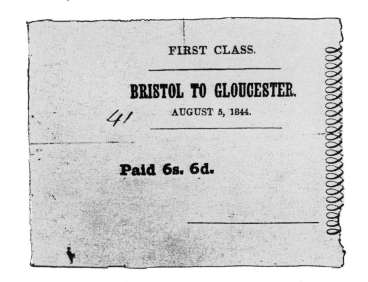

FIRST CLASS.

BRISTOL TO GLOUCESTER.

41

AUGUST 5, 1844.

Paid 6s. 6d.

DISPOSALS OF B&GR LOCOMOTIVES

No.		Selling price to Brassey £	Brassey's name	Withdrawn
1	Broken up 1856			
2	5/1856 sold to Thomas Brassey, contractor for working N. Devon Rly	1000	Venus	8/1870
3	Broken up by 9/1851			
4	6/1855 sold to Thomas Brassey, contractor for working N. Devon Rly (price included 10 wagons and brake van)	1180	Exe	by 1862
5	11/1855 sold to Thomas Brassey, contractor for working N. Devon Rly	1200	Tite	8/1870
6	5/1856 sold to Thomas Brassey, contractor for working N. Devon Rly	1200	Barum	8/1870
7	Withdrawn 1/1853 after boiler explosion outside Bristol 8.1.1853 broken up 7/1854			
8	8/1856 sold to Thomas Brassey contractor for working N. Devon Rly	1000	Star	4/1877
9	11/1855 sold to Thomas Brassey contractor for working N. Devon Rly	1200	Mole	8/1870
10	8/1857 sold to Thomas Brassey contractor for working N. Devon Rly	1200	Dreadnought*	by 1862†
11	8/1857 sold to Thomas Brassey contractor for working N. Devon Rly	800	Defiance*	10/1867

(Defiance was badly damaged in a fire at Crediton, 8th October, 1862, but was repaired by end of year.)

* Name stamped on splashers.

† Dreadnought was stopped with cylinder and firebox trouble when taken over by the LSWR in 1862. It was sold for £950 to Mr Sharp, a Falmouth contractor, in June 1863, but not removed from Barnstaple until the following September as this gentleman had some difficulty in finding the money.

Until 1880, express engines at Bristol were Nos. 820–829 of Kirtley's '800' class 2–4–0s, but that year were replaced by Johnson 2–4–0s Nos. 1282–1296, Nos. 1297–1301 joining them three years later. Until 1888 Bristol engines did not normally work north of Birmingham, but that year, 2–4–0s Nos. 1295 and 1296 hauled the 'Scotch Express' to Derby. Three 2–4–0s were still at Bristol, in 1933. 1892 saw the appearance of 4–2–2 engines of the '115' class at Bristol, but these were replaced by 4–4–0s within a few years, but until the mid-1920s could still be seen as train engines on reliefs as well as acting as pilots. Nos. 673 and 679 ended their days on locals to Gloucester.

Goods traffic was worked by double-framed 0–6–0s, supplemented in 1892 by new '1357' class 'express goods' engines of the same wheel arrangement. In 1875–6 new 0–4–4Ts Nos. 1274–1281 arrived to work local passenger services. From the 1930s the 0–4–4Ts were joined by class '3P' 2–6–2Ts.

The 'Devonian' and the Newcastle Mail were hauled by class '3' 4-4-0s, lighter expresses being headed by class '2' engines of the same wheel arrangement. The class '3s' were remarkably speedy, steady runners and well-liked by their crews. The first three Compounds at Bristol were Nos. 1023-1025 which arrived in 1924, joined by Nos. 1026-1028 and finally by Nos. 1029-1031, all with 7 ft diameter driving wheels. 'Patriots' appeared on the line in 1931 and during World War II headed the heaviest train, the 7.40 am from Bristol, always made up of 15 bogies. 'Black Fives' and 'Crabs' also worked expresses. On 15th October, 1937 'Jubilee' class No. 5660 *Rooke* reduced the running time from Leeds to Bristol from 4 hours 45 minutes to 4 hours 13 minutes.

In 1943 ex-Somerset & Dorset Sentinel shunters Nos. 7190 and 7191 worked at Avonside Wharf, Bristol. 'Royal Scot' No. 46120 *Royal Inniskillin Fusilier* appeared at Bristol in February 1949. A train between Gloucester and Bristol hauled by a Beyer-Garratt 2-6-0 + 0-6-2T class was restricted to 40 wagons because of limited siding accommodation and the length of the locomotive itself took more siding space than a conventional engine. A Garratt appeared on the line daily in March 1950. At the Bristol shed it occupied the whole of a short pit road. Ex-LNWR 0-8-0s occasionally appeared on freight workings.

Several Caprotti valve 'Black Fives' worked between Bristol and Derby. They ran freely, but never had the 'guts' of a piston valve engine climbing or accelerating. 'Britannia' class Pacifics were rare on the line. BR Standard class '9' 2-10-0s Nos. 92004, 92007, 92221 and 92248 arrived at Bristol shed in 1961.

Until weight restrictions over Stonehouse Viaduct were eased in 1927, 'County' class 4-4-0s were the heaviest GWR engines permitted and so these worked that company's Birmingham-Bristol expresses. Once the LMS civil engineer was prepared to accept 'Saints' over the line, there was no need for the 'Counties' and their withdrawal began. In actual fact, due to their balancing, the 'Counties' had a far more severe hammer-blow at speed than the four-cylinder 'Stars' or 'Castles', but dead weight per axle was the only thing which counted with LMS Midland Division civil engineers.

'FOREIGN' ENGINES

In 1941 rebuilt SER 'F1' class 4-4-0s worked some Bristol to Gloucester passenger services; SR 'K10' class Nos. 135, 137 and 138 were shedded at Barrow Road during World War II. These engines worked goods to Clifton Down and also the 10.38 am goods to Gloucester. On one memorable occasion a 'K10' stalled with its train on Barton Street Crossing, where the railway was not to exceed a three minutes occupation. The outcome of this incident was that these SR engines were banned from working to Gloucester.

When driver Tom King of Barrow Road shed arrived on duty one Monday morning, the locomotive foreman told him to take No. 137 out of the shed and halt it at a spot where the road had a slight curve and there wait for district superintendent Whitaker, his assistant, and a footplate inspector. The latter arrived while Tom King was taking the engine out of the shed and informed him that they intended testing the gear, as on the previous

Saturday a Gloucester driver had been unable to move at Berkeley Road and caused a serious delay as single line working had to be instituted. It was fortunate that King was told this, for he then knew what to do. There was a snag with the steam reverser on No. 137. If the engine was put sharply into reverse gear it jammed, and the locomotive could not be moved.

When the trial began, that is exactly what Tom King did and for some 20 minutes or so when told to drive the engine forward or backward, the engine remained firmly rooted. Having satisfied them that the engine was immovable, King was told to take No. 137 back to shed which he immediately did, no one asking how he could move the immovable!

'S11' class 4−4−0s, Nos. 396−404, classified '2P' like the 'K10s', from 1941 onwards occasionally worked from Bath to Bristol or Gloucester on goods trains from Bath LMS.

For a couple of weeks an SR 0−6−0, believed to be a Wainwright class 'C', was at Barrow Road. For its first job, driver Tom King was told to use it to bank the 7.40 am express up to Fishponds. As his fireman raised steam, the pressure gauge never moved off the 80 lb. mark. On examination, Tom King found that the pressure gauge received its steam from the top of the boiler gauge glass and some mischievious person had shut off this supply. The same thing must have happened to another LMS driver who was shunting with this engine at Fishponds and could not understand why the engine appeared to be growing weaker while the gauge showed plenty of steam.

LYR 0−4−0ST 'Pug' No. 11212 arrived in the 1930s to work the Avonside Wharf branch and this class remained there until 1961 when Nos. 51217 and 51218 were replaced by 204 hp diesels Nos. D 2134 and D 2135.

In 1959 York 'B1s' regularly worked through to Bristol on Saturdays with the 12.48 pm ex-York, returning the following day with the 4.45 pm from Bristol to Bradford. A 'V2' class 2−6−2 sometimes appeared on this train, but technically was not cleared for the route. 'B1s' also worked through summer Saturdays trains from Weston-Super-Mare to Sheffield. Other ER engines recorded have been 2−6−0s of the 'K1' and 'K3' classes; and '01' and '04' 2−8−0s. Class 'J39' 0−6−0 No. 64930 from Northwich shed arrived at Bristol with a down freight on 23rd August, 1959 and No. 64789 of the same class from Spital Bridge shed, Peterborough, on 11th October, 1959.

In the early sixties 'Peak' class diesel electrics took over express working, HSTs were placed on some South-West to North-East services from 1st October, 1981 running to ordinary schedules, and from May 1982 with reduced journey times.

LOCOMOTIVE WORKING

E.L. Ahrons gives an exciting account in the *Railway & Travel Monthly* for September 1914, of racing between Gloucester and Standish.

> That night on our arrival at Gloucester, where we were due at about 11 pm. I slipped off our engine and ran down into the Midland Railway barn, which at that time adjoined the equally picturesque one-platform shed which did duty for the Great Western passenger station. My object was to discover if the Midland express to Bristol, then due to leave, was anywhere in the neighbourhood. It could hardly have been better, for there was the Bristol train almost ready to back out prepara-

tory to the start from outside, and there was also the well-known jovial and smiling countenance of one of the best known Bristol men in charge at the locomotive end of the train. But to my astonishment it was not his usual engine of the '1290' class, but in place thereof I saw a complete stranger to the West, engine 816, which I recognised as a well-known Leeds acquaintance with a big reputation on the Carlisle road. Now I knew a little about these '800's, having had many journey and not a few timings behind them, and I realised that we were up against the toughest proposition that we had hitherto encountered. Moreover he had only 'equal to' 12 on, and we had 13. On my duly reporting the results of my investigation to my driver, he was somewhat inclined to scout the idea of any Midland engine being quite good enough for us.

Anyway we started out for Swindon, took matters easily over Tramway Crossing, round the sidings, and through the cutting, in order to give the Midland man time to back out and restart, so that when we emerged from the cutting on to the straight where the two lines converge and begin to run parallel to each other, we were some 200 yards or so in front of 816 and the Bristol express, with the full intention of increasing our lead before we parted company at Standish Junction, seven miles on. And we ran too! for in spite of the slow start out of Gloucester we covered the 12 miles to Stroud in 14 minutes start to stop. But it was all to no purpose, for at Naas Crossing 816 was alongside, and literally seemed to fly past us, so that at Haresfield station the tail was opposite to us, and before we reached Standish the Midland tail lights were disappearing behind the trees in the direction of Stonehouse. My driver looked absolutely dumbfounded, and was a much sadder man for two or three days. All that he asked, when he got to Swindon, was 'What did you say was the number of that Midland engine?' Nor would he be consoled with the information that we had been beaten by one of a class that were then second to none in the country, and that the Midland man had had one coach less than we had. I often wondered but could never discover what was the actual speed of 816 that night from Gloucester to Stonehouse. I frequently saw and chatted with the same Midland driver at more or less irregular intervals during the next three years, but he 'did not know,' and I rather suspect he did not want to say.

In 1940 ammunition ships were arriving at Avonmouth and visits from the Luftwaffe made it imperative that the ships were unloaded as quickly as possible. The Sheffield area assembled a train of 59 empty vans to be sent to Avonmouth and headed it with Millhouses star engine Compound No. 1079 which they had nicknamed 'Bluebird'. When he stopped for water at Cheltenham, driver Bill Bagnall went back to the station box on the platform and informed the signalman, 'Tell Gloucester Control that if they are turning us through Eastgate, we shall want a clear run.' Bill continues his story in his own words:

Speed was down to 30 mph over Tramway Crossing and the distant for Barton Street being seen to be clear meant that the signals at both California and Painswick Road were also green. Speed could now be increased to get a run at the bank. Realising the power of this 'Bluebird' of a Compound, I even had her on compound passing California and was most surprised to find that she was easily going to skip by Tuffley with the charm and grace as if she had a 9 coach express.

Naas Crossing and Haresfield were soon behind and Standish was now well aware of why he had to keep a 'cross-lighter' [goods train headcode] standing at his 'pegs'. Stonehouse, Frocester and Coaley saw little of the 60 vehicles as we sped by at near express speed. The green automatic signal at Wick meant that Charfield had cleared the road by shunting a fitted train which caused a pair of Bristol men to fume somewhat when informed that they had to stop there to give the special a clear run. Just beyond Wickwar Tunnel was the disused limestone kiln, an indicator to railwaymen that the summit of the incline had been reached.

Yate came and went and now there was anticipation as to how the train was to be hauled to Avonmouth. Westerleigh obeyed the instructions that had preceded the train from its start: 'Clear road wherever possible'. In the brake van the guard, who had up to now marvelled at the running of the train, was now in something of a quandary as somewhere the train would have to be reduced in length to conform to the regulations governing the route from Kingswood Junction to Avonmouth. This line involved several gradients which restricted weight and train length to a much lower level than that of his present train. When he saw the distant signal off for Westerleigh North he was in two minds whether to stop the train by lifting the setter in his van. He decided to let events take their course.

Mangotsfield North and station were passed at a little over the 30 mark. Fishponds distant was green, and a signal I have never seen off before – the right hand distant under the Fishponds starter. This meant that Kingswood Junction was clear to Ashley Hill. The guard thought, 'It's out of my hands now.'

At Ashley Hill Junction the distant was on for Montpelier and here we came to a stand for the first time since leaving Cheltenham.

I realised that climbing the gradient to Clifton Down from a standing start would be a severe test for the compound.

Off came the signal, I opened the regulator and away we went, speed being so good that by the time they were passing through Redland I decided to slip her over into compound working and she, that marvellous No. 1079, took them over the top. We sped down through the tunnel, through Sea Mills and over the hill at Horse Shoe Bend and on to our destination, Avonmouth.

Working loose-coupled freight trains demanded skill to avoid a coupling breaking and even with care, experienced men could have a divided train. A colleague of the men mentioned, describes an event which occurred about 1928.

One dark night driver Fred Davey and fireman George Millward were working an empty wagon train from Westerleigh Sidings to Gloucester. The load was 58. In the brake van was guard George Cummings, nicknamed 'Slippers' because it was a well-known fact that he took off his boots and put on slippers for comfort when in his van.

Approaching Charfield, the distant signal was at danger, but as they neared the post it was cleared. Fred allowed the engine to drift, and after passing through the station, gave the engine steam. Almost at once there was a jerk and the two men on the footplate, both with wide experience, deduced that a break-loose had taken place. Stopping would have been dangerous as they could have been struck by the break-away wagons, so they carried on to Berkeley Road where the signals were at danger owing to Charfield having noticed that the train was running in two sections.

When they stopped, Fred said to George, 'Nip down and see how many we still have.' George was back quickly to explain to Fred 'We ain't got any – we're light engine.' Fred whistled for the signal and drew up to the box where it was agreed that they would go back to Charfield and there decide what action to take when they knew the position of the rest of the train.

Off to Charfield they went and noticed that the train had become almost stationary a few yards short of a bridge. They proceeded on to Charfield and decided to go right road and push the lost portion to Berkeley Road.

They crossed over and came back behind their train. You can just imagine the shock to George Cummings when an engine pulled up behind his brake . . . but his surprise was even greater when he found that it was the engine which was, in his opinion, on the front of his train!

The ensuing chat elicited that he knew nothing of the break-loose and had decided that the engine was doing badly for steam as it almost stopped twice before the final halt. George decided that the footplate crew would eventually contact him and let him know what was going on. It was amazing at the calmness with which old guards accepted such happenings.

It was not standard practice, but when heading a passenger train a fireman could fill his firebox at Temple Meads and this would last to Gloucester; this method rather surprised Great Western men learning the road.

One crew at Barrow Road, sent to drive BR Standard class '5MT' 4−6−0 No. 73025, returned saying that no engine with this number was on shed. The office asserted that it was, unless stolen. On investigation it was found that the engine had '73025' on one side and '73155' on the other. What had happened was that when in the shops for cab repair, the damaged section had been replaced by that from the withdrawn No. 73155!

Loads of Passenger Trains Bristol to Fishponds 1st October, 1945

Class of Passenger Engine	1	2	3	4	5	5X
Load in Tons	165	225	270	300	345	380

When passenger trains from Bristol are worked by the above classes without assisting engine in front and exceeding the load above, they should be assisted in the rear from Bristol Engine Shed Junction.

Loads of Freight Trains Bristol to Fishponds 1st October, 1945

Class of Freight Engine	1	2	3	4	5	6	7	8
No. of wagons Express Frt	23	28	33	40	44	48	53	58
No. of wagons Through Frt	27	32	39	47	51	56	62	68
No. of wagons Mineral train	16	19*	23*	28*	30*	33*	37*	41*

* A 20 ton brake van is required when train is unassisted. If assistance is required: 'Trains must be brought to a stand on the Lawrence Hill Junction side of Engine Shed Sidings Signal Box until the assisting engine has joined the train'.

Loads of Mineral Trains Fishponds to Bristol

Class of Freight Engine	1	2	3	4	5	6	7	8
No. of wagons	28	34	40	48	53	58	64	70

LOCOMOTIVE DEPOTS
Bristol

Initially eight broad gauge engines were shedded at Bristol, the small original B&GR depot being replaced at a cost of £20,000 by a standard MR roundhouse with 42 ft diameter turntable in 1873. A roundhouse design had the advantage that no engine could be struck by another while a driver was oiling it, thus moving the motion and risking an injury. In 1874 a 4-road fitting shop was added to the rear. A 60 ft turntable was installed in 1927 at a cost of £3,212.

The Midland Shed was coded 8, its sub sheds were Bath and Thornbury. In 1935 LMS motive power depots were reorganised into locomotive supply and repair and garage schemes. Bristol was a main, or concentration, depot (Code 22A), with Gloucester (22B), Bath/Radstock, Templecombe, Highbridge, Wells and Tewkesbury as its garage depots. The object of the scheme was to effect economies by reducing the stock of parts at the smaller depots.

A water softener, mechanical ash plant and coaling tower were installed at Bristol in 1938−9. If coal was wanted from the tower, the number of the engine was dialled, a lever pulled, and the coal fell. Two roads were situated below the hopper so that two engines could be coaled simultaneously. Coal wagons were moved by capstan. One wagon, not checked before tipping, proved to be filled with pipes. Great difficulty was experienced extracting them from the hopper.

Italian prisoners-of-war were employed at the depot during World War II. They lived in the ambulance hut and worked labouring in the yard. They are chiefly remembered for placing bait in a box and trapping starlings to eat. They also made stew from tins of cat food.

The depot was transferred to the Western Region in February 1958, and was re-coded 82E; it closed entirely on 14th October, 1965.

Gloucester

Initially three broad gauge engines were allocated to the first shed, opened on 6th July, 1844. This was replaced by a second on 8th July, 1850, this latter being on the roundhouse plan and situated between the broad gauge transfer shed and the passenger station. It cost £4,085 and an additional £965 for smithy and stores. The turntable was enlarged in 1869 and an additional 50 ft table installed in the yard. As this second shed stood on land required for a new through passenger station, it was closed on 2nd July, 1894 and replaced by a roundhouse at Barnwood. This became Midland Railway Code 7. A new 55 ft turntable was installed in 1935. In February 1958 it became WR shed 85E and was re-coded 85C in January 1961. It closed on 4th May, 1964, its locomotives and men transferring to the ex-GWR Horton Road shed.

Sub-sheds of Gloucester at Dursley, Evesham, Nailsworth, Stroud, Tewkesbury and Worcester. Engines at Gloucester were mainly for local work and tended to be elderly. After 1880, '170' class 2−4−0s Nos. 180−8 were shedded there, assisted by '230' class No. 231. Compound 4−4−0s Nos. 1000 and 1001 arrived in the 1930s, as did ex-LYR 0−6−0s Nos. 12131, 12140 and 12141.

For more humble duties, in 1874 when the MR leased the Swansea Vale Railway, nine 0−6−0STs were sent to Gloucester for dock shunting. 0−4−0Ts kept at Gloucester for working the High Orchard branch were Nos. 1428A and 1429A in 1892; Nos. 1505, 1519 and 1522 in 1914, and No. 41537 in the BR era. From 1895, ex-Severn & Wye Railway 0−6−0Ts Nos. 1606 and 1608 were at Gloucester, remaining there until withdrawn in 1923 and 1924.

Chapter Nine

Rolling Stock

CARRIAGES

Stothert, Slaughter & Co. provided the carriages under a 10 years' contract, and this helped the B&GR by avoiding an outlay on carriages, carriage shed and repair shops. The vehicles were painted brown and lined and trimmed like GWR carriages. The first class coaches had three compartments, with four individual seats each side. The second class had four compartments each holding 12 passengers. Built by W. Williams, a Bristol coachmaker, they had iron frames and the springs were of a new design and constructed on Buchanan's patent. 'The carriages were remarkably easy and pleasant, and the oscillation, even at the highest speed, was very slight.' In June 1844 Slaughter was asked to 'board up the second class carriages to make them the same as the second class composites'.

The coaches had six wheels of 4 ft diameter and 'for the poorer class of travellers', there was standing accommodation open at the sides and having no roof. They were equipped with a Stanhope − corrupted not inappropriately into 'Stan-up' − lever brake. Slaughter's were paid 1d. for their hire.

Twenty coaches were used at first, but in May 1845 the Bristol & Birmingham Directors asked for four first class and five second class and two composite carriages. In August 1846 two more composite carriages were required and W. Williams of Bristol tendered for £320 each excluding wheels, axles and axleguards, but apparently the B&GR misunderstood Williams reply and he wrote again saying he could not tender. Eventually the tender of Adams & Allcock at £424 10s. 0d. exclusive of wheels, etc. was accepted.

The Midland Railway purchased the stock from Stothert, Slaughter & Co. in July 1845, and in August, tenders were obtained for a further two broad gauge composite coaches. The following February, the Board drew McConnell's attention to 'more effectively closing the second class carriages on the Bristol & Gloucester line'. In March the extra door was made in the third class carriages. In April 1847 Kirtley was instructed to order six first class and eight second class broad gauge carriages from J. Knight at £420 and £280 respectively.

The 'Report on Railway Carriages for Conveying Third Class Passengers at or under One Penny per Mile' published in 1849 was not very complimentary regarding B&GR rolling stock. 'No night lamp; one door only on each side. A sight of the country is confined to the passengers who are fortunate enough to get near the door. No provision is made for the admission of air in bad weather, when the doors and windows are closed. This badly lighted and badly ventilated carriage carries fifty-four passengers.'

After conversion of the line to narrow gauge, the broad gauge stock was no longer required and some was sold to the Bristol & Exeter Railway (B&ER).

MR No.	MR Class	B&ER Class	B&ER No.	Year condemned	B&ER Alterations
124	1st	1st	26	1873	To 2nd class 1866, No. 10
125	1st	1st	25	10.1875	To fish van 1.1865, No. 29
126	1st	2nd	54	9.1871	–
127	1st	1st	24	1.1870	–
128	1st	2nd	55	1874	To fish van 2.1865, No. 30
129	1st	1st	27	4.1868	–
73	composite	2nd	51	7.1873	–
74	composite	2nd	49	1.1867	–
75	composite	2nd	52	1870	–
Not known	composite	2nd	Not known	Not known	–
147	2nd	2nd	11	1.1867	–
246	3rd	2nd	50	1867	–
247	3rd	2nd	53	1864	–

From 2nd August, 1897 new train sets were used on the 1.25 pm Bradford–Bristol and the 2.05 pm Bristol–Bradford, a third set being kept as a spare. Their cost totalled £16,800. Each set consisted of a 6-wheeled guard's van, 12-wheeled 3rd class coach, 12-wheeled dining car, 6-wheeled kitchen car with luggage space, a 12-wheeled compo. 1st class dining car and a 12-wheeled brake compo. Within a few years the roofs were painted in sans-serif letters with the words 'Bradford, Leeds, Birmingham & Bristol Express'.

In pre-Nationalisation days, Bristol–Newcastle trains were composed of LNER and LMS stock on alternate days.

WAGONS

The goods wagons were also hired from Stothert, Slaughter & Co. They had only four wheels instead of the six which were usually provided on the broad gauge. GWR six-wheeled mineral wagons weighed 5¼ tons and held 9 tons of coal and were not suitable for direct trade with collieries. In March 1844, Francis Fry was requested to order 30 coal wagons from William Harris, Darlington (or 50 if delivered in Bristol at £50 each), and 30 wagons from George Hennett. Harris was Engineer to the Stockton & Darlington Railway and designed a hopper-shaped broad gauge wagon with moving floor to let the coal drop down, facilitating discharge which was difficult with flat-floored coal wagons. In order to save dead weight, Harris made them almost the size of narrow gauge wagons. Their construction was weak, with resulting high maintenance costs. Coal owners disliked these wagons as the depth of the body broke the coal. They held 4½ tons.

In August 1844, Hewitt, a Bristol coal merchant, hired 50 coal wagons and 40 more were ordered from Hennett in September. In August 1844, Hammond was asked to submit a drawing of a flat-floored coal wagon and in March 1845 Stothert, Slaughter were asked to provide 40 extra goods wagons.

B&GR trucks weighed 4 tons 19 cwt. and carried '7 fat beasts', while narrow gauge cattle trucks weighed 3 tons 10 cwt. and carried '6 fat beasts'.

The Midland Railway purchased Stothert's stock in July 1845, when it totalled 82 goods vehicles.

In December, Hamer had an order for 100 goods wagons with double brake at £68 10s. 0d. In October the following year, tenders were obtained for 40 coal wagons, 20 to be suitable for general purposes. The tender of Lloyds, Foster & Co. for 20 at £79 15s. 0d. was accepted and also that of W. Williams, Cheltenham Road, Bristol, for 20 wagons at £71 each. Then in December, Williams asked for permission to withdraw his tender and 20 were ordered from Isaac Marshall & Sons at £84 10s. 0d. each. In October 1847, the still-increasing traffic demanded more wagons, and 30 narrow gauge wagons were ordered to be immediately prepared for broad gauge traffic. Two years later there was another shortage of wagons as those in use were being overloaded. To ease the situation, another dozen were ordered.

After narrowing of the gauge in 1854, the older broad gauge wagons were broken up and the rest sold.

Class '1F' 0–6–0T No. 1878 at the LMS Gloucester goods yard in 1924 with the Gloucester Railwaymen's District Coal Supply Association wagon built that year. The association purchased coal in bulk and supplied it to members at a fraction of the price charged by coal merchants. *Author's Collection*

Class '4F' 0−6−0 No. 44211 hauling an up freight train passed Kingswood Junction, April 1956. The line on the right leads to Clifton Down and Avonmouth. A down freight can be seen on the left. *W.H. Harbor/Author's Collection*

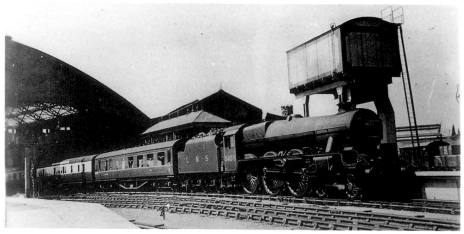

'Jubilee' class 4−6−0 No. 5658, later named *Keyes*, at Temple Meads with an up express, *c*.1935. *Miles Davey*

LMS Compound No. 1048 arriving at Temple Meads with a down express, August 1936. On the left a GWR Pannier tank is shunting. *M.J. Tozer Collection*

Chapter Ten

Permanent Way and Signalling

In June 1842 the Directors agreed to longitudinal baulk sleepers being adopted, as they were more economical in the first cost and needed less maintenance. A depression in the iron trade in 1842 allowed the B&GR to buy the rails cheaply. The bridge rail weighed 56 lb./yd and was fastened to the baulks by screw bolts passing through the flanges at regular intervals into elm or other hardwood planking about 1 in. thick and 8 in. wide, which was laid on the longitudinal baulks. Felt was placed between the rail and the planking. The sleepers were kyanised (saturated in bichloride of mercury, a preserving process invented by Dr Kyan), and the bolts, screws and exposed surface of the woodwork tarred. The lowest tender for the rails was accepted, that of Thompson & Foreman of the Rhymney Iron Company: 7,000 tons of rail at £6 7s. 0d. a ton delivered in Bristol, though later the price was reduced to £6 3s. 0d. The rails were sent in weekly shipments of 250–300 tons to St Philip's wharf and then travelled up to the Bristol & Gloucestershire Railway, though some went up the Avon & Gloucestershire and 1,500 tons for the northern section of the B&GR was shipped to Stonehouse.

George Hennett, who had surveyed the line, offered to provide all materials, except the rail and lay the permanent way for £2,840 a mile. Brunel discussed it with him and managed to get the terms reduced to £2,760, so the permanent way cost the company only £3,886 per mile. Hennett delivered the baulks in about 11,000 loads in the first six months of 1843. The beams were required to be 14–15½ in. square, at least 22 ft long and averaging 30 ft or more. Rails for the Standish to Gloucester section were made by the Coalbrookdale Company.

In March 1846 the Great Western agreed to supply the B&GR with a few tons of rails at £12 2s. 6d. a ton for use in emergency. The permanent way was maintained by contract, 50 per cent more being paid for the mixed gauge section, and in August 1846, William Fleetwood gave notice that he was to discontinue this between Standish Junction and Bristol. In September, J. Paton & Sons were given the contract for £2,940 per annum. Peters, Brown and Guest maintained the broad gauge lines at Gloucester in 1846 for £160 per annum. From 2nd August, 1847, William Guest took over all the permanent way contracts for £110 per mile for the Bristol to Standish section; the Coalpit Heath branch, Gloucester dock, and the broad gauge sidings at Gloucester station.

In 1844 each policeman had a three-aspect lamp showing red (danger), green (caution), white (all clear). Each policeman had to 'take care that his Lamp is well trimmed and kept clean, and the Glasses quite clear and unbroken'. He had to show the signal until every carriage or truck had passed him. 'In all cases the Policeman signalling is to stand on the opposite side of the Railway, that he may be quite conspicuous to the Driver and Fireman, as well as to the Conductor and Guards'.

A red light was to be shown to a train arriving within three minutes of another; after three minutes a green light was shown until 10 minutes from the time the first train had passed. 'In the Day time, Arms are to be used to denote the same Signals; the two Arms raised over the head, when a Train or Engine shall have passed within Three Minutes in the same direction along the Line; and one Arm raised over the head, when it shall have passed more than Three Minutes but within Ten Minutes.'

It was the duty of every policeman, as soon as he came off duty, to report to the superintendent of the station any disobedience of signals given by him. In the event of an accident, the policeman was required to show a red light and go back and stop any train until he met another policeman to whom he communicated the same instructions or until he had proceeded a mile from the place of the accident where he remained displaying the danger signal.

At each station and gated level crossing were disc and crossbar signals and also flags (or lights at night) on a separate mast. A red flag by day, or red light at night meant stop; a green flag or light meant caution, slacken speed. A white light showed all clear.

'A Full Disk will only be seen when the Line is perfectly clear and no Engine shall have passed for Three Minutes previously'. 'The Flag Staff, to shew Signals for Engine or Trains, on the Down Line, is always on the South and left-hand side of the Down Train; and for the Up Line is always on the North and left-hand side of the Up Train.' 'In case of a Fog, both Day and Night signals must be used simultaneously.'

The Bristol & Birmingham Railway rule book of 1845 mentions an arrow-shaped vane signal, green one side and red on the obverse.

In 1845 block signalling was installed in Wickwar Tunnel and throughout from Gloucester to Bristol between 1869 and 1873.

There were quite a number of signalling peculiarities in the Bristol area. At St Philip's there was double line block working on a single line, the home signal at Lawrence Hill really being the outer home for St Philip's. There was a ground frame at the passenger station to allow an engine to run round. If Lawrence Hill down distant was off, this indicated a clear road to St Philip's station. Similarly Lawrence Hill up distant was sited at the end of St Philip's platform under the home and, if the former was off, indicated that a train had a clear road up the bank. Between Lawrence Hill and Temple Meads all distants were fixed at Caution.

Staple Hill, not a block post, had an intermediate block signal at the end of the platform and worked from Fishponds, while at the east end of the tunnel was a down intermediate block signal worked from Mangotsfield. Both these intermediate block signals were unusual in being mechanical, for, because of the distance usually involved, most intermediate block signals were motor-worked, or colour light.

At Westerleigh a slotted lever at each signal box allowed a train to set back to the up or down side respectively.

Fumes drifting from the tunnel obscured Wickwar down starting signal situated in the approach cutting and so it was replaced by a colour light. For a similar reason, the semaphore up distant near the south portal of the tunnel was replaced about the same time.

The introduction of power signal boxes at Bristol and Gloucester caused the old manual boxes to be closed. Barton Street Junction signal box built in 1894 was one of the MR's few gantry boxes. Painswick Road Level Crossing signal box has been preserved on the Avon Valley Railway, Bitton.

Dates of sections coming under Gloucester Power Signal Box

Engine Shed Junction–Tuffley Junction/California Crossing	25–26.5.1968
California Crossing–Naas Crossing	10–12.8.1968
Tuffley Junction–Standish Junction	14–15.9.1968
Standish Junction–Charfield	12–14.10.1968

Dates of sections coming under Bristol Power Signal Box

Charfield–Yate South Junction	18–20.10.1969
Yate South Junction–Westerleigh Junction, and new layout	17–18.1.1970

Gloucester station in May 1961 with No. 44591 being closely inspected by the young train spotter.   *H.C. Casserley*

The Charfield accident on 13th October, 1928 seen from the overbridge after much wreckage had been cleared. Damaged goods wagons are in the foreground and a steam crane on the down road is assisting with the rescue work. *Author's Collection*

Charfield goods shed, 14th October, 1928, the day after the accident. A steam crane is still at work on the left. *Miles Davey*

Chapter Eleven

Accidents

The first mishaps were only minor, such as the engine of the inaugural train being derailed outside Gloucester on the opening day (already described).

On 4th May, 1846 there was a derailment at Stonehouse caused by a subsidence in the embankment. On 27th June, 1846 the 5.30 pm up express from Bristol to Birmingham narrowly missed disaster midway between Wickwar and Berkeley Road when one of the leading wheels of the locomotive flew off and buried itself deeply in the embankment. The locomotive and tender jumped 15–20 yds across the down line and the first coach was badly smashed and all were derailed, but no injuries were caused to passengers.

A collision took place at Westerleigh on 4th December, 1846 between the 8.15 am passenger train and a train of empty coal wagons which was imprudently allowed to be shunted across the main line when the passenger train was due. The signalman was convicted with a penalty of 40s. or one month's imprisonment. On 1st April, 1848 a ballast train on a siding at Wickwar was not shunted clear of the main line. The magistrates fined the driver £2 and the guard £1. They were also dismissed from the company's service together with the fireman.

On 4th April, 1848 a Bristol & Birmingham express collided with a GWR goods at Standish. The Great Western claimed the B&BR driver was in the wrong and charged damages against the company. It brought to light the fact that the GWR policeman at Standish stopped the B&BR goods for GWR passenger trains, but not GWR goods for B&BR passenger trains.

In 1853 an unidentified broad gauge B&GR 0–6–0 left Bristol for Gloucester at 8.10 pm with 20 goods wagons. Just before reaching Fishponds it stalled on the gradient of 1 in 75. The driver decided to divide the train, so he and his fireman made their way towards the brake van in order to scotch the wheels of the rear wagons. The engine had only been standing for a couple of minutes when its boiler burst, sending the top half, including the dome, over some lineside cottages, to land some 500 yds distant. The enginemen, now towards the rear of the train, escaped injury. Both safety valves were set to blow off at 65 lb. and it is believed that the explosion was caused by defects in the iron boiler.

An excursion train was run weekly from Gloucester to Weston-super-Mare and as it approached Mangotsfield North Junction on 30th August, 1886, a down goods on the line towards Bath mistook the signalman's indication for the passenger train to proceed, as a sign for him to set the freight back. The excursion engine and its first two or three coaches passed the junction safely, but then the brake van of the reversing goods train fouled the main line and coach after coach scraped the van, to the detriment of their side panels and stepboards.

No passenger was injured apart from Kathleen Organ, a 13-year-old girl who had her hand out of the window and received a cut. After it received a dressing at Bristol General Hospital, she was able to continue with her journey, the superintendent at Bristol kindly extending the validity of her excursion ticket for a few days in case she wished to recuperate at Weston-super-Mare. Less fortunate was James Quick, the passenger guard, whose protruding ducket was ripped off, causing him to be thrown to the van floor. His mouth was badly injured and he received cuts to his head. Taken to the same hospital as the girl, he lay unconscious for about ten hours.

The line's most serious accident occurred on 13th October, 1928. It was about an hour before sunrise on a still autumn morning and signalman Harry Button was on duty in his box at Charfield station. After a telephone conversation with his control office at Fishponds, he decided to shunt the 9.15 pm Oxley Sidings, Wolverhampton to Bristol fitted freight in order not to delay the 10 pm Leeds to Bristol mail which was shortly due.

From his box on the down platform, Button watched GWR 2–6–0 No. 6381 slowly reverse its load of 49 loaded wagons and brake van into the refuge siding. While this was happening, two other trains were approaching Charfield: the 4.45 am up empty freight train from Westerleigh to Gloucester, and the 10 pm Leeds to Bristol mail.

He pulled off the signals on the up line for the empty freight to pass through, but the three down signals were against the mail because the interlocking would not permit them to be cleared until the Bristol-bound goods train had completely reversed into the lay-by siding.

The down mail passed the previous signal box at Berkeley Road Junction travelling at its normal speed of 60 mph. Button watched the goods back-shunting and kept glancing at his track circuit indicator for the mail's approach as he wanted to change the points as soon as possible and pull off the signals in order not to delay it a moment longer than necessary.

Imagine Button's horror when he realised that the mail had failed to stop at the outer home signal! Simultaneously, the up empty freight passed through Charfield station. He knew three trains were about to collide and there was nothing he could do to prevent the catastrophe.

Class '3' 4–4–0 No. 714 and its mail train grazed the last two wagons of the Great Western goods train setting back into the siding and struck the right hand rear end of the locomotive tender pushing that train. This resulted in No. 714 being derailed and coming into contact with the wagons of the passing up empty freight and then ploughing to a standstill on its side. Its tender, together with GWR No. 6381, became wedged under the over-bridge and, with the wreckage of the destroyed wagons, blocked the forward movement of the mail coaches. This resulted in the first five vehicles of the mail piling themselves on each side of, but chiefly under, the bridge in an inextricable mass of steelwork and timber wreckage, the momentum of the whole train being absorbed in the destruction of the first five vehicles.

The wooden-bodied coaches were lit by gas and so all the ingredients for a holocaust were present. Fire started in the wreckage and rapidly grew into a furnace with the result that eventually the first seven vehicles of the mail, two loaded wagons of the down goods and a number of empty wagons were burnt out.

Immediately after the collision, Harry Button informed the control office at Fishponds that a serious accident had occurred and asked that ambulance appliances and breakdown trains should be sent from Gloucester and Bristol.

Station master Brown, on his way to the station, saw flames at the bridge and arranged for a chain of men with fire buckets to check the blaze on the station side of the bridge, and also provided axes and bars to assist helpers in releasing some of the passengers. He telephoned Wootton-under-Edge police station asking them to advise doctors, nurses and ambulances to be sent quickly, to summon assistance from fire brigades at Dursley, Stroud and Bristol, and also to warn the Bristol hospital to prepare to receive casualties.

An ambulance belonging to Messrs Lister & Co. arrived from Dursley and a train with ambulancemen and equipment from Bristol. Stretcher cases and other injured passengers were placed in this train. Meanwhile, fire brigades had arrived and were at work. The Bristol brigade arrived in 35 minutes and pumped water from a stream 100 yds distant, but despite the efforts of the various teams, the blaze was to continue for 12 hours.

Out of a total of approximately 60 passengers travelling on the mail, 16 lost their lives and 24 suffered injury; in addition, 13 Post Office sorters as well as the driver and fireman of the GWR goods and both guards of the LMS trains were hurt. Of the total of 41 injured, 11 were taken to hospital and detained. Medical opinion on the bodies of the victims recovered from the wreckage was, as far as could be determined, that death was caused by multiple injuries received, and not from burning.

And the cause of the accident? Colonel J.W. Pringle, inspecting officer for the Ministry of Transport, said that he could not accept the accuracy of the statement of driver Henry Aldington or fireman Frank Want that they saw a green light at the distant signal. He therefore concluded: 'The responsibility for this collision rests upon Driver E.H. Aldington, who, in my opinion, passed the distant signal for Charfield in the warning position, and subsequently the outer and inner home signals at danger. To a minor extent, I think responsibility rests also upon Fireman F.C. Want.' Colonel Pringle recommended that Automatic Train Control be installed to prevent misreading of signals; that coaches be made stronger and the desirability of abolishing gas lighting in coaches.

At the inquest on 30th and 31st October, the coroner interpreted the jury's verdict as one of manslaughter and committed driver Aldington for trial on that charge. He appeared before the local magistrates on 20th and 30th November. They found there was not a *prima facie* case and he was discharged. On 1st February, 1929 at Gloucester Assizes, the jury returned a formal verdict of 'Not Guilty'.

The press thought this a very proper decision, for both men declared with convincing emphasis that, although they had admittedly failed to see the home signals, they saw the distant perfectly distinctly showing clear. Aldington said that owing to the misty conditions, he had crossed the footplate and was standing behind his fireman peering ahead. They had both seen the green light about 50 yds away, Want immediately exclaiming, 'He's got it off, mate'. After the collision in which he miraculously escaped serious injury, driver Aldington helped in the rescue work until the fire made it hopeless.

The signal certainly could have shown green if a heavy object had been placed on the wire, or the wire deliberately pulled by someone between the signal box and the signal, but whether this did in fact happen will probably never be known.

There is one other strange feature about the accident. Two charred and unrecognisable bodies, possibly of children, were among the victims and their identity was never established. It seems incredible that two children should travel on a night express without someone being aware of the fact, yet nobody came forward to claim them, and they could not be connected with any of the other victims of the accident. They were buried in a grave in Charfield churchyard on the hill above the railway, together with those of ten other named victims.

A rather less serious accident occurred on 15th October, 1932. While using a pricker loosening clinker in his firebox in the vicinity of Coaley, George Millward was knocked off his engine when the tool struck a lineside object. Severely injured, he was placed on a railway stretcher, but this was too long for Messrs Lister's ambulance and the railwayman too ill to be transferred to Lister's stretcher, so the handles were cut off the railway stretcher so that it would fit into the ambulance. George Millward survived this accident.

On 30th September, 1949, class '5MT' 4–6–0 No. 44745 was heading the 1.58 pm parcels train from Derby to Bristol and as it passed Westerleigh Sidings at high speed round about 7.30 pm, came into contact with the open door of a banana van stationary on the up line. The fireman, sitting on a seat overlooking the side of the cab, received a blow on his head and died two hours later.

Inquiries elicited that railway staff had been known to open doors of banana vans to search for fruit overlooked when unloading, and the Ministry of Transport Report placed responsibility for the accident on the unknown person who had failed to fasten the door on the last occasion it was opened; superelevation on the curve caused the insecure door to swing open.

Memorial in churchyard at Charfield to those killed in the crash. Photographed on 3rd August, 1981.   *Author*

Chapter Twelve

Staff Matters

Guards, policemen and porters had to be not less than 5 ft 8 in. nor more than 35 years of age when appointed to the B&GR. Clerks had to be not over 35 and had to provide £300 security. A goods clerk's salary was £100 per annum and a passenger clerk's £90. It was pleasant to know that 'No fee or gratuity is permitted to be taken by any guard or porter or other servant of the company under pain of immediate dismissal.'

In June 1844 the weekly wages were: guards 21s.; switchmen 18s.; policemen and porters 15s. plus a suit of clothes each year and an allowance for keeping them in repair. All employees were required 'to be dressed in white fustian, or other suitable clothes, which are to be clean every Monday morning, or on Sunday when he may be required to work that day'. In June 1845 passenger guards' wages were increased to 25s. a week and to 26s. in October. In February 1847 they were brought into line with the Midland Railway's rates of pay – first guard, 27s.; second, 24s. Goods guards' wages were reduced to 24s. in January 1849. Guards were expected to assist porters and to be on duty half an hour before the train left. In January 1847 the wages of the three brakesmen for the coal traffic at Bristol, were raised to 17s. a week. In July 1847, porters' wages were brought into line with the Midland's and raised to 17s. a week.

When the station duties were completed, the station clerk rang a bell and the guard gave the driver the starting signal, which was a white flag by day and a white light at night. Gatekeepers were instructed to keep the gates open to the railway and not to open a gate for a carriage within five minutes of the expected arrival of a train, or within 10 minutes if a herd or flock wished to cross.

In February 1851, Ivey the Berkeley Road station master was £70 2s. 10d. in arrears. He was given a month's notice and told that if the sum was not paid within a week, his sureties would be called on. He paid his debt in the allotted time. His salary was £80 per annum less the house rental of £15.

If a driver failed to give a satisfactory explanation of a train's lateness, for every minute over five he was fined 2d. a minute and any premiums due to him for coke saving, disregarded.

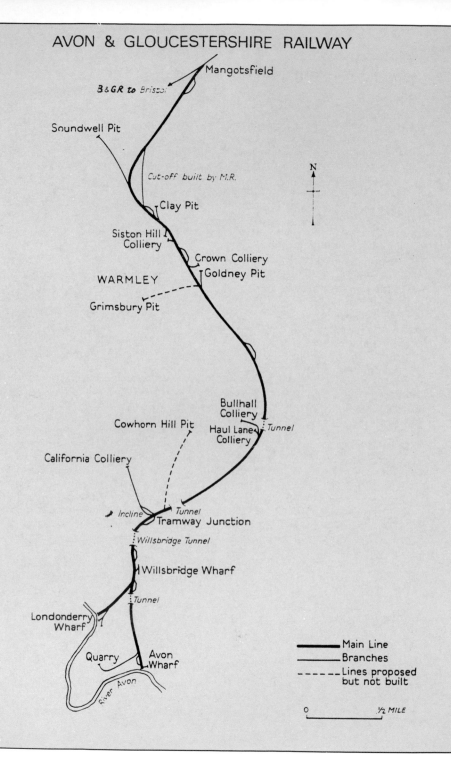

AVON & GLOUCESTERSHIRE RAILWAY

Mangotsfield

B&G.R to Bristol

Soundwell Pit

Cut-off built by M.R.

Clay Pit

Siston Hill
Colliery

Crown Colliery
Goldney Pit

WARMLEY

Grimsbury Pit

Bullhall
Colliery

Cowhorn Hill Pit
Haul Lane
Colliery

Tunnel

California Colliery

Incline
Tunnel
Tramway Junction

Willsbridge Tunnel

Willsbridge Wharf

Tunnel

Londonderry
Wharf

Quarry
Avon
Wharf

River Avon

N

Main Line
Branches
Lines proposed
but not built

O   ½ MILE

Chapter Thirteen

The Avon & Gloucestershire Railway

In 1803 the Wilts. & Berks. Canal contemplated building a railroad from Pucklechurch and Coalpit Heath to the Avon near Keynsham. The Kennet & Avon Canal (K&ACC) was willing to support the scheme, but nothing seems to have come of the project. On 3rd November, 1812 John Blackwell, Engineer of the K&ACC, said in his report to the Committee of Management of the K&ACC that he had surveyed the line from Coalpit Heath to the Avon and found the ground not favourable to a railway because it was hilly and 'Throws the line very crooked'. The length of his road would have been about 10 miles and would have cost £3,500 per mile. He suggested the works could be completed in a year and 200 tons of coal would pass daily, in addition to other commodities (200 tons at 2d. per ton/mile, 300 days in year = £500 per mile per annum).

The sum of £20,000 had to be subscribed to apply for an Act of Parliament, and the K&ACC agreed that if the sum was not subscribed by 10th February, 1813, the plan would be shelved. In fact not enough was subscribed, and this course was adopted.

In 1827 as we have seen, the scheme to connect Coalpit Heath with Bristol was revived as the Bristol & Gloucestershire Railway, and, in December, two members of the K&ACC committee asked their company's solicitor, Thomas Merriman, to communicate with the Bristol & Gloucestershire Railway proposing that a branch to the Avon would be a great advantage. On 13th February, 1828 the K&ACC agreed to subscribe £10,000 towards the project. John Blackwell estimated the total cost to be £20,226 11s. 2d. The Act allowed £21,000 in £100 shares and borrowing powers for £10,000.

The 10 promoters of the Avon & Gloucestershire Railway were:

Robert Bruce	Frederick Page
James Heygate (Jnr)	Thomas Shaw
William Hughes	Robert Sutton
Thomas Merriman	William Taunton
Samuel Mills	John Wells

W.H. Townsend surveyed the Bristol & Gloucestershire section, and H.F. Cotterell the A&GR section. The line rose from 22 ft above sea level at the Backs, Bitton, 198 ft above sea level at Mangotsfield, a distance of 5 miles. The steepest gradient was 1 in 76 from north of the Bristol to Bitton road to north of the Bitton to Warmley road. Blackwell surveyed the Bristol & Gloucestershire line of tramroad from Coalpit Heath to Rodway Hill, Mangotsfield, and considered it 'very objectionable and expensive'. He suggested a very much better route which could be laid from Coalpit Heath to the Avon. In view of this survey, the K&ACC Western sub-committee could not recommend the K&ACC to make application to Parliament in that session 'for execution of a railway to the Avon connected with one so defective'.

Ten days later, on 18th January, the Bristol & Gloucestershire Engineer admitted a rise of 10 ft each mile from Coalpit Heath to Rodway Hill, and said it was to be reduced to 5 ft. The K&ACC approved this modified line and said they would support the Bristol & Gloucestershire in Parliament and apply for a branch from Rodway Hill to the Avon. A special meeting of the K&ACC on 13th February, 1828 agreed to subscribe £10,000 to the A&GR 'from the operation of which Works, your Committee confidently anticipate a considerable accession of Tonnage and a reduction of Price in the Articles of Coal and Pennant Stone'.

The Act 9 Geo. IV, cap. 94 was passed on 19th June, 1828, all costs and expenses of the Act being paid by the K&ACC. Unlike the 'Bristol' Act, where there was no mention of locomotives, the A&GR Act said that steam engines should consume their own smoke. Contracts for building the line were let to Charles Pearce, James Woodward and Thomas Wilkins.

Following the purchases of the A&GR shares in private hands, on 21st July, 1829 the K&ACC agreed to borrow £20,000 on promissory notes under the authority of 49 Geo. III, cap. 138 (K&ACC Act of 3rd June, 1809) at 4½ per cent to help build the A&GR. Blackwell said that the extra cost of building bridges of sufficient width for double line would be £200 to £300 more and it was thought advisable to do so in case the line was ever doubled, though in the event, only single bridges were built.

In October 1829, five branches were proposed:

Shortwood Colliery from junction at Mangotsfield (67 ch. Built by Bristol & Gloucestershire).
Soundwell Colliery from Siston Common (43 ch. Built by A&GR).
Grimsbury Colliery (30 ch. Never built).
Willsbridge–Londonderry Wharf (25 ch. Built by A&GR).
Wick Limestone Rocks, from Backs (3 m. 4 ch. Never built).

Further trouble broke out between the Bristol & Gloucestershire and the A&GR late in 1829 when Osborne & Ward, solicitors to the former wrote a letter expressing disapproval of the A&GR's Shortwood and Londonderry branches as 'being a violation of the arrangements and understanding between the respective committees'. The Londonderry branch would have given the A&GR a competitive route to a point on the Avon nearer Bristol than the wharf at the Backs and avoided the tolls at Keynsham lock. The A&GR said that it was unaware of any understanding, but met the Bristol & Gloucestershire on 9th June, 1830 when the outcome was that the latter undertook to build the line to Shortwood immediately.

Some wayleaves were difficult to obtain and John Blackwell and H.F. Cotterell surveyed some deviations. In 1830 a scheme for deviations and branches was put forward and 'An Act to alter the Line of the Avon & Gloucester [sic] Rail Way, to make certain Branches from the same and to amend the Act for making the said Rail Way' was passed on 30th July, 1831, 1 & 2 Will. IV, cap. 92. It allowed several deviations giving a straighter main line (including the making of Willsbridge tunnel); the raising of further capital of £15,000 and some branches:

Bone Mills to Cowhorn Hill pit (60 ch.).
Redfield Lane to Hole Lane pit (6 ch.).
Crown Inn, Warmley to Grimsbury pit (30 ch.).
Siston Common to Soundwell coal works (43 ch.).

Only Hole Lane and Soundwell branches were actually built; Hole Lane used to be spelt Haul Lane.

The first meeting in the Backs office, Bitton, was on 27th October, 1830. John Blackwell, Engineer to the K&ACC and also the A&GR said he wished to be relieved of his railway duties as they interfered with his canal work. He thought that as the works were in a forward state, W.H. Eastwick could complete them without his assistance as long as two of the three members of the Western sub-committee of the canal met Eastwick at the Backs office every fortnight to check the accounts. Eastwick was paid a quarterly salary of £37 10s. 0d.

The committee examined a 'pattern wagon', approved it and travelled in it from the Backs to Hole Lane colliery, making the first of frequent inspection trips by the committee. At their meeting on 9th November, they were told that Willsbridge tunnel had a mistake in the level and required deepening, and also that the two bridges had not been built according to the plans. On 17th November Blackwell thought that a speed of over 6 mph might injure the railroad, so Eastwick was ordered to see that this limit was kept and to dismiss offenders. By 1st December, 1830, the wharf at the Backs, Avon Wharf, was nearly ready; rails had been laid and the crane was waiting to ship coal (300 yds of rail had been laid in the preceding fortnight).

George Jones, Chairman of the Bristol & Gloucestershire visited the works as he had heard rumours that works on the A&GR had stopped until the spring. Finding that the tales were false, he promised to push on with his works, but thought that coal could not get to the junction at Mangotsfield until the spring. Hole Lane were ready to send coal from the nearest point on the line then open, and six wagons were forwarded to be loaded on 30th December, 1830. As the Londonderry branch had yet to be built, Hole Lane were allowed to send coal from Avon Wharf to Bristol without paying more tonnage to the K&ACC than they would have from Londonderry.

In January 1831, Whittuck wanted to make a branch to his colliery at Soundwell. He offered, if the A&GR would lay the line, to pay £450 towards the cost. The committee replied that they were not empowered to engage the company in any expense, but would give him every facility to do the work himself, allowing him to use A&GR wagons and the railway free of tolls to carry out the work.

On 10th January, 1831 the railway was usable for more than 2½ miles. In February Hole Lane stopped sending down coal, but rails had been laid to Siston Hill pit and coal started coming from there on 16th January. Eastwick and Robert Bruce (Chairman of the sub-committee), made a trip from Siston to the Backs in under 45 minutes. It is believed that horses pulled wagons up the line, but were only used on the downward journey in passing loops or where the incline was shallow.

The severe winter months caused the embankments and cuttings to slip and impeded the laying of rails. However by mid-March 1831, the mileposts were erected every ¼ mile up to 3¼ miles and the blocks and rails laid for a ¼ mile further on and Hole Lane was sending down coal again. Woodward, the Bristol & Gloucestershire contractor, promised to finish the northern section of that line over which the A&GR had running powers from Coalpit Heath by 1st August.

In the first week of May, Hole Lane sent down 15 wagons of coal but the A&GR was troubled by vandalism. Robert Brown and Richard Arnold, surveyors to the A&GR, said that on the two previous Sundays, people had broken locks and chains holding the wagons to the rails and rolled them down the railway.

The cost of the line up to 7th May, 1831 was £41,996 0s. 8d. The K&ACC borrowed another £10,000 on promissory notes that year, and a further £10,000 the following year. In May, Eastwick threatened that if he was not given the opening date of the Bristol & Gloucestershire, he would inquire if they had indeed spent the 40 per cent of their capital the Act required on the northern part of their line. This threat had the desired effect, and the manager of the Bristol Company said that rails would be laid connecting to the A&GR within three months, so Eastwick let the matter drop. On 5th June, 1831 the connection with the Bristol & Gloucestershire was made, but the line beyond, to Shortwood and Coalpit Heath, was not ready for traffic.

In July the A&GR found that traffic was being impeded by lack of a branch at Hole Lane, and a loop or branch at Siston Hill was desirable. At the beginning of August, one wagonload of Shortwood coal was loaded at Rodway Hill, and a wagon of Soundwell coal loaded at Siston Hill. The length of the 17 turnouts on the line, including the one to Hole Lane sheds, was 1 mile 72 yds and the length of the main line 4 miles 1,552 yds making a total length of 6 miles 1,624 yds in addition to 400 yds of temporary road to the quarry at the Backs.

In August there was some trouble with the works settling. On Warmley embankment temporary wooden sleepers replaced the stone blocks until the settlement was complete, and Oldland embankment was found so unsafe that a massive retaining wall had to be built of stone from a heap above Willbridge tunnel. Before coal could come from Shortwood or Coalpit Heath, it was reiterated, a branch or turnout was essential at Hole Lane and Siston Hill.

On 17th October, Bruce and Eastwick rode down the line from Shortwood pit to the Backs in under an hour. Only 200 yds was necessary to connect the Shortwood branch to Coalpit Heath, and the Soundwell branch was complete. The expense of laying it was £716 13s. 4d., which was repaid to the K&ACC by the colliery owner. By 9th November the Hole Lane branch was finished (it cost £80 7s. 5d. for materials) and was in use. The branch to Warmley pit was begun and finished in four weeks; the £31 15s. 0d. expense entailed in building the branch was repaid to the K&ACC.

'As the wagon went along the Railway it appeared firm and fit for working, but between the junction and Shortwood, one or two turnouts must be put in before the trade can come down without interruptions.' Urquhart, resident surveyor of the Bristol & Gloucestershire said in October 1831 that if he received the order for the turnouts immediately, the coal might come down from Shortwood by the end of the month. Hole Lane used the line five days a week and 21 wagons of coal came down from Soundwell and 45 more tons were sent down the line en route for Swindon in December. The northern portion of the Bristol & Gloucestershire was opened by 17th July, 1832, though no record of the exact opening can be traced. The total cost of the

A&GR had been £52,710 6s. 11d.; the income in August 1832 was £358 2s. 10d. The opening of the A&GR led to a reduction in the price of coal along the K&ACC by three to four shillings. At the end of November, Eastwick reported that nearly 3,000 tons of coal had come down the railway that month and all the company's wagons were fully employed.

Curiously enough, the Coalpit Heath Company had a greater income before the opening of the A&GR than after it, even though the quantity sold was 60,000 tons instead of 18,000 tons. The reason was that they had expended more capital in making new works. On 28th July, 1834 the A&GR agreed to give the Coalpit Heath Company a reduction of 4d. ton on coal going east and 2d. going west, in addition to the 4d. reduction in toll and 4d. off hire of wagons. The receipts from the opening of the A&GR until 31st May, 1835 were: tonnage, £3,041 15s. 3d.; hire of wagons, £1,072 6s. 5d.; rent, £989 15s. 0d. a total of £5,103 16s. 8d.

On 9th September, 1835 a letter was read to the General Purposes Committee from W.H. Eastwick offering to rent the A&GR together with wharves, cranes and wagons for three years at £350 per annum and to keep the whole in repair. If the yearly tonnage reached £900 he offered to pay £600, but if it failed to exceed £400 he would pay only £200. The committee rejected his proposition. Eastwick's salary was £150, and at this time it was reduced to £60 per annum plus £10 per cent on the gross amount received for goods passing on the railway. For example, from 29th May, 1836 to 30th November, 1836, tolls amounted to £302 6s. 3d., so his percentage was £30 4s. 8d. He was allowed the use of the company's wagons for £20 a year and kept them in repair.

The branch to Londonderry was staked out early in September 1832; work began in December and was completed the following July, except for the weighbridge which was not put in until August. The wharf was opened in the first week in October 1833. The branch had cost the A&GR £1,541 15s. 7d. but was on a different account from the rest of the line. At Londonderry the Coalpit Heath Company built a 70 ft long shed for storing 200 tons of small coal. Hole Lane also built one of the same dimensions. At the back of the sheds, a double line was laid so that wagons could discharge straight into them. The Shortwood pit also had a coal shed. The wharf had two berths – one for large and another for small coal. In the first two months it shipped 735 tons. On 26th April, 1834, Eastwick said that the small coal shipment from the wharf in five days was 243 tons 7 cwt. and 59 tons 18 cwt. of this was shipped in one day. At the Backs during the same period, 628 tons 14 cwt. had been shipped and the previous week 1,025 tons 12 cwt.

By 9th May, 1837 the committee was getting worried about declining traffic since the opening of the Bristol & Gloucestershire in August 1835, and decided to confer with Coalpit Heath regarding a definite supply of coal to its line. The Bristol company was carrying three times the quantity of coal the A&GR was taking from Coalpit Heath, and barges on the Avon at Bitton were waiting, and asking for an equally large quantity as was being sent to Bristol. Less than half the coal from Coalpit Heath went down the A&GR in March 1837 compared with what had gone down in a similar period in 1834. Upwards of 15,000 tons were shipped from the Backs in March 1836, and in March 1837 only 7,300 tons.

The Coalpit Heath owners said they hoped complaints would soon stop, as two more pits were to be opened. Eastwick proved that wagons intended for the Backs were loaded for the Bristol line; the preference was given because Hewitt's son (Hewitt was the Coalpit Heath agent), was the agent in Bristol, and he had a percentage on the quantity sent to Bristol. Robert Bruce said it was unfair that the K&ACC had incurred an outlay to connect the colliery to the river, and although much coal was brought up, they did not have it for their eastern trade. To help improve traffic, in August 1839 the railway tonnage on coal going east along the Avon was remitted provided the colliery owners reduced their price by 6d. ton at the pithead. In November, ashes and cinders going down the A&GR were allowed the same drawback as coal, provided they went east.

Fortunes of the railway were declining, and by 1843 the average loading had fallen to 204 tons in 46 wagons a week, and this remained the average figure until 1850.

Most of the money loaned had been paid off (the last loan was paid on 12th February, 1851), but it was impossible to pay off the capital expenditure. In June 1843 the K&ACC resolved that the £45,000 bad debt due from the A&GR be written off. A shareholder, Charles Brand, wrote pointing out to the committee that writing off a debt was merely charging another account with it and not getting rid of it. He proposed that amounts be credited to a sinking fund, which would be transferred to the credit of the railway, so that year by year, the railway debt would be paid off. In September, Brand's plan was adopted.

Meanwhile, the Bristol & Gloucester was completing its new broad gauge line from Westerleigh Junction to Standish Junction. In 1843, Hennett, who had the Bristol & Gloucester Railway permanent way contract, paid the A&GR £500 for the use of its line while carrying out his contract, and the B&GR paid the A&GR £400 for the use of its wharf for storing Hennett's permanent way materials. Coal traffic from Westerleigh to Mangotsfield was suspended from 5th June, 1844 while the line was 'mixed', but by 29th July, a single line of narrow gauge was finished and ready for use by the A&GR; how this came about will now be described.

When the B&GR converted the Mangotsfield to Westerleigh section to broad gauge, it became the first mixed gauge in the country. The 35 lb./yd fish-belly rails were laid between the broad gauge rails, and the narrow gauge lines laid 2 in. above broad gauge level, so that at crossings, the only gaps necessary were in the narrow gauge rails. The narrow gauge rails were spiked to transverse sleepers, 8 in. by 4 in. by 6 ft. which did not interfere with the B&GR longitudinal sleepers. The A&GR complained to the Board of Trade about the interruption of their traffic. When Major-General Pasley made an inspection on 5th July, 1844, he said that the new arrangement was better for the A&GR as there would be less interruption from two sets of rails than from the previous arrangement of one with turnouts. Horses would be able to travel over the 2⅝ miles of common route in less than an hour, and Pasley added that he had observed that:

. . . railway trains drawn by horses seldom or never travel slower than the rate of 3 miles an hour. Hence as the Bristol and Gloucester Railway Company proposed to run six passenger trains on week-days, at intervals of not less than two hours and twenty minutes between succeeding trains, it is impossible that collision can take place, provided that the Avon & Gloucestershire railway trains shall be so arranged as always to follow one of the Bristol & Gloucester passenger trains in a short time after the latter shall have passed on the junctions, whether travelling northwards or southwards.

Blackwell said that the A&GR trains being restricted to following B&GR passenger trains would impede the free and uninterrupted communication with the coalpits. When asked by Pasley, Blackwell was unable to give him any traffic figures, so Pasley, reading between the lines, thought traffic must be inconsiderable, as if it had been great, locomotives would have been used. In fact, Pasley thought it would be a good thing for A&GR trains to run at fixed hours. The A&GR was unreasonable in wanting to run its one or two daily trains at any time of the day or night and he recommended that A&GR trains wait for and follow B&GR passenger trains at intervals of 2 to 15 and not exceeding 20 minutes. He said that as long as the A&GR used horses, B&GR passenger trains must not run at closer intervals than 1½ hours. Later Pasley withdrew this suggestion, and said that the only safe way of working was for the A&GR to have an independent line, but the A&GR found the expense of this more than the traffic was worth. Pasley suggested the two companies came to an agreement, but this failed, and no more traffic travelled from Coalpit Heath to the A&GR.

In the summer of 1844, the A&GR made complaints about the B&GR obstructing traffic, and the B&GR submitted a proposition for working not more than two A&GR trains daily over the Coalpit Heath to Mangotsfield line.

Bristol & Gloucester Railway Office,
Exchange Buildings,
Bristol.

26 August, 1844.

My dear Sir,

In accordance with the undertaking at our conference on Tuesday the 20th instant at your Board Room, Sydney Place; I beg to submit on the part of the Company the two following propositions for the conveyance of Coals from that *part of the Railway* used *as and for Passenger traffic* from *Westerleigh* to the junction of the Avon Branch.

First. In the wagons of the Avon Company at eight pence per Ton for the whole distance including the five pence now paid. *Second.* This Company to provide wagons calculated to run on the wide gauge and also to undertake charge of widening the Rails upon your lines to receive such wagons; to be delivered at the commencement or junction of your railway as proposed No. 1 – your undertaking to return the empties at the same place – at ten pence per Ton including the five pence now paid.

I remain
Yours respectfully,

Geo. Jones.

J.N. Sanders, Esq.

This letter was not the sort of proposition the Western sub-committee was expecting to obviate the obligations the B&GR had to comply with in 2 & 3 Vic. cap. 56 Sec. 3 (see page 11). It said that the first proposition did not provide for carriage of coal from Coalpit Heath to Westerleigh, and yet contemplated a payment to as great an amount as it cost to convey the coal from Coalpit Heath to the A&GR. The B&GR was silent on the subject of compensation for loss by stoppage of trade on the A&GR while the conversion was being carried out. In October the B&GR agreed to lay a second line of narrow gauge rails and work was completed the following month, though not to the satisfaction of the A&GR which thought the work imperfect.

The A&GR sent a memorial to the Board of Trade on 19th November. Major-General Pasley was busy elsewhere and sent his assistant Captain Codrington to investigate on 27th November. Of Keynsham Junction he wrote:

> I found the work of a very objectionable character. The pairs of rails of each gauge are not laid upon the same level and the crossing (not) effected by switches or points in the usual and only proper manner, but the narrow gauge is kept 2 in. above the broad, and the waggons are intended to pass over the latter without any other guide than a check-rail on one side, while there is no rail at all on the other for a distance of 21 feet; besides which, the work is executed in a cobbled and imperfect manner, and is, in my opinion, dangerous from the liability of the waggons to get off the rails and block up both lines.

Codrington tested some empty wagons across the up turnout (the other had been lifted), and found that they made an 'irregular jumping motion' and believed loaded wagons would have been de-railed. Instead of the sleepers being held in the ballast, they were lying on it, and the ballast was so uneven that in several places the sleepers hung from the rail instead of supporting it. He thought the line quite unfit for a horse to draw a load along.

He found a very crude arrangement for getting broad gauge wagons from the up line into the sidings at Shortwood colliery: four narrow gauge rails had to be lifted out and then replaced after the passage of the broad gauge wagon. For this they were left loose in their chairs, 12 ft being without chairs or any support. Their removal caused an inadmissable obstruction, especially as it was not done by a special man, but just the brakesman of each train. There was a similar arrangement at Westerleigh Junction and there was no procedure by which trains of each company could know how far ahead was the preceding train.

Pasley commented that the turnouts and crossings were imperfect and dangerous as 'no stationmen or signals are appointed or intended at the turnouts'. In July he had expected the two companies would work 'in a spirit of conciliation', but instead of that they were hostile. He thought the only safe way of working would be for the B&GR to lay down heavier rails so that the A&GR could use locomotives, or else build independent tracks for the A&GR (i.e. not inside the broad gauge rails as then existed), but the B&GR found the expense of this more than the traffic was worth.

In November 1849, Tugwell, on behalf of Coalpit Heath colliery, asked why the working of the A&GR had not been perfected according to the agreement entered into. The committee replied that they were ready to co-operate with the colliery owners in 'endeavouring to get that portion of its Railway now under the management of the Midland Railway Company put into a proper state for traffic'. In August 1850 Blackwell tried to obtain tenders for leasing the A&GR, but no one wanted it. In December the K&ACC reiterated that they were ready, as they had always been to co-operate with the coal owners to re-open the A&GR. On 1st July, 1851 the K&ACC undertaking passed to the Great Western Railway by transfer deed dated 29th July, 1852, made under the terms of the GWR Act No. 1 of 30th June, 1852. In 1851 the K&ACC had said that there was hardly any revenue from the A&GR; by this time many of the pits had been worked out, or else flooded, and abandoned. Section 33 of the GWR (Additional Powers Act), 5th July, 1865, finally authorised the Great Western to abandon the whole or part of the A&GR; but the track still remained and the last entry in the A&GR account book was January 1867. Hole Lane pit was the last to put traffic on the line.

In August 1873, one Gabriel Goldney applied for leave to lay down a crossing so that he could take coal from his Crown colliery to the Midland Railway's station at Warmley on the Mangotsfield to Bath branch. W. Simpson, in his letter to the K&ACC's Engineer's office at Bath GWR station, said that he saw no objection to Goldney's tramway crossing the A&GR and taking out a couple of rails 'as it has not been used for the last 20 years'. In return, Goldney was asked not to mine the seam he owned just under the A&GR rails, nor require them to pay compensation as the MR had to do, to prevent him undermining their Warmley station.

However, in 1876, California colliery at Oldland was re-opened and in 1881 the line from the colliery southwards was repaired at the expense of the lessees, who in return were allowed three years use of the line free of tolls.

On 2nd October, 1885 the Kennet & Avon Canal reported on the state of the A&GR:

Purposes of the Act
   In June 1828, an act was obtained for the purposes of making and maintaining a Railway, or Tram Road, for the passage of waggons and other carriages from Rodway Hill in the Parish of Mangotsfield in the county of Gloucester, to the river Avon in the parish of Bitton in the county of Gloucester with a view of opening a convenient communication from several extensive collieries and stone quarries on the line and in the neighbourhood to the City of Bath, and various other places in Somerset, Wilts and Berks.

Course and Length of Line
   The line which is about 4 miles long, begins at Avonside, in the parish of Bitton, where a Wharf Weighbridge and Tipping Stage have been constructed for the purpose of loading minerals and goods into Boats on the River Avon for conveyance to Bath, and places on the Kennet and Avon Canal, and to places on canals in connection with it, and runs through Willsbridge, Oldland, Siston and Warmley to Mangotsfield, where formerly siding accommodation was provided and Traffic was transferred from the Bristol and Gloucester, (then a Broad gauge railway) from the 'coal pit heath' and other Collieries and works on the line.
   A short branch of about 25 chains in length is also constructed from the River Avon at Londonderry in the parish of Bitton, which forms a junction with the main line at a point 40 chains from the Avonside terminus.

At Londonderry a wharf sidings and loading stage are constructed and a crane and weighbridge are erected, so that convenient means are provided for loading and unloading traffic that may be received on the Avon from or be despatched Westward to Bristol, and other places.

Gauge and Permanent Way

The line is laid on a gauge of 4'8½", the rails are single 'T' headed, and weigh 30 lbs to the yard, and they are fixed by means of a light iron key, into chairs (weighing 8 lbs each) on stone blocks (except where these for repairs have been substituted by wooden blocks). There are three tunnels on the line. No 1 which is at Willsbridge is 6½ chains long, is lined with masonry throughout, and in section gives a height of 9ft 8inches from Rail level to crown of arch, and a width between side walls of 10 ft 2 inches. No 2 Oldland Tunnel is 7 chains in length, cut through the rock and unlined, except for 30 yards where the Midland (Bath & Mangotsfield) Railway passes over it, the height from Rail level to crown of arch is 9 ft 3 inches and width in lined protion between walls is 9 ft 2 inches – No 3 Tunnel is situated near to Cowhorn Hill, but is not lined. It is 72 yards long, is 8 ft 2 inches from rails to top of arch, and 8 ft 9 inches wide. A bridge at Oldland which crosses the tramway has a headway of only 8 ft from rails to crown of arch with a width between walls of 8 ft 8 inches, all the other bridges are at least 9 ft high and 9 ft wide. The height of Tunnels and Bridges might if required, be increased by lowering the rails and underpinning the walls, but increased width could only be obtained by their complete reconstruction.

Between Avonside and Warmley, except at places where turnout sidings occur, the widths of cutting and embankments at rail level, vary from 9 ft to 12 ft between Warmley and Mangotsfield, the line is chiefly surface formed through common land, the width is not clearly defined, but the original plan shows the land taken, to have been 40 to 45 ft wide.

In 1864 the Midland Ry Company obtained powers under which they diverted the tramway near Rodway Hill, but there is no record in my office (Mr Hart), of their having paid anything in respect of land taken or for easements, neither have I obtained any information of the disposal of Land abandoned, when diversion of Tramway was made – I am not aware whether the Company acquired the land through Siston Common absolutely or only surface rights over it for their purposes, but a clause in the original act (pages 8 & 9) enables Lords of the Manor and other persons to negotiate and convey so that they may possibly have purchased the land occupied absolutely. I direct attention to this as important whenever a sale of the undertaking is determined upon.

Capital

The capital authorised to be raised under the original Act of 1828 was £21,000 in shares of £100 each, and £10,000 by mortgage of the undertaking, and in 1831 a further Act was obtained to make certain deviations of the tramway and to construct certain branches which are described as 'the Cowhorn Hill branch' the Haul Lane Branch, the Grimsby Branch and the Soundwell Branch and this Act conferred upon the Company, further capital powers under which they were authorised to raise on mortgage or otherwise, a sum not exceeding £15,000 and to pay interest thereon at a rate not exceeding £5 per centum per annum. I am unable to state how much of the authorised capital was expended upon the undertaking, but the probabilities are the powers of the Act of 1828 were wholly exhausted, but seeing that only the 'Haul Lane' and the Soundwell branches were constructed, the powers conferred by the Act of 1881 may not have been fully exercised.

Present State of Repair

The Tramway between Avonside and Warmley, and between Londonderry and Warmley has been recently overhauled and is now in a fair state of repair, there is one turn out siding about midway between the places named and another at Warmley, and the line could now be used for the transmission of a considerable amount of traffic over this portion if necessary. The recent repairs were executed at the request of a Mr Coslett, who conducts some brick and tile works at Warmley, but since the line was put in working order his use of it has been so limited that the tolls received from him have not half paid interest on the sum expended. Between Warmley and Mangotsfield the tramway is in a very defective condition, in several places. The rails have been removed for repairing other parts of the line, and the transverse sleepers laid down by the Midland Company in about 1865 when they diverted the tramway would require to be entirely renewed, before Traffic on that part of the line could be resumed.

There is now no means of exchanging Traffic with the Midland Company at Mangotsfield, probably for the sufficient reason that the Bath and Mangotsfield Ry now meets the requirements of the district, so that for the tramway there is no traffic to be exchanged.

Sources of Traffic

The tramway runs through a well populated district, but it is well served by the Midland Co. for conveyance of every description of Traffic, so that Tramway Traffic must be derived from works and coal pits to which it affords the *only* outlet, and these for the most part have been either abandoned, or are in an unsatisfactory working condition.

The Paper Mills at Avonside have been overtaken by financial difficulties before they were completed. The Oldland Colliery works have to contend with water in the lower seams, so that their output is only equal to sales at the pit, and the Warmley Pit is now, and has been for two years or more contending with faults in the working seams, so that there is no immediate probability that any Traffic will be derived from these sources.

Some Brickworks at Warmley are doing a good business, and the Tramway runs close to the Kilns, but they are also near to the Warmley Station, and the manufactured goods are sent away by the Midland Ry.

There is also a Pennant Stone Quarry about half a mile from Warmley, which at ,some future time may be developed, the stone is good in quality, but at present all that is quarried is used in the neighbourhood of the Quarry between Warmley and Mangotsfield, the coal pits and Spelter Works have been abandoned, so that future Traffic prospects are not encouraging.

Present Income from Property

The rents derived from the letting of Tramway Banks, Cottage Property &c and House at Avonside amount to £82:6:8 per annum.

Negotiations for sale of Tramway

The propriety of disposing of the Tramway has in past years been considered by the Committee, the latest negotiations are referred to in the minutes of the Committee of 26th November 1879, where is appears that Mr Gabriel Goldney desired to acquire it, and in pursuance of that object made an offer of £1200 for the tramway with the houses and cottages and land appertaining to it.

At the same meeting Mr George F. Fox of Hamleaze, Keynsham approached the Committee for terms of sale, or lease of the Tramway, with the view of making it useful to the district through which it passes. Both negotiations were barren in results, Mr Golding's offer was declined and Mr Fox's never became a definite proposal.

Conversion and Extension of Tramway

The prospects of utilizing the Tramway, wholly or in part, extending it at both ends and converting it into a permanent Railway, do not appear worthy of much consideration, for although it passes through a fairly populated district, and at one time might with advantage have been converted, the necessity for conversion passed away when the Midland Company constructed the Bath and Mangotsfield Railway, which traverses the whole district, and running almost parallel to the Tramway affords all the accommodation at present required. The only extension that suggest itself is the construction of a line about 6 miles long from Patchway to Warmley and from Avonside across the river to join the Great Western Main line between Keynsham and Saltford for the purpose of affording a shorter route and increased facilities for the conduct of Traffic conveyed through the Severn Tunnel from South Wales in an eastern direction, but the immediate necessity for a nearer route will be supplied when the new loop line at Bristol is completed and the future Traffic requirements will be better met both as regards the providing a shorter communication and the affording accommodation to a district now without a Railway by the making a line from Patchway to Malmesbury.

Sale of Tramway

From the foregoing details the Committee will be able themselves to determine whether or not the sale of the undertaking should be attempted, for my own part, I do not think that purchasers for the Tramway as a whole could be found at present at a price that could be entertained, and if it were sold piecemeal as land and materials, the property would have to be sacrificed, therefore notwithstanding its failure to earn a traffic income, seeing that the income derived from other sources protects the Company from a monetary loss, I am of opinion that their interests will be best promoted by continuing their ownership, and retaining any advantages that future necessities may develop.

I have conferred with Mr Balding and Mr Hearne on the subjects of this report, and I am authorised on their behalf to state that in their view the sale of the Tramway is undesirable.

(Signed)   Charles F Hart

Kennet & Avon Canal
Engineer's Office
2nd October 1885   *Devizes*

In August 1892 about 60 tons of coal went daily from California Colliery to the Avon and an additional 18 tons from the colliery to Willsbridge coal wharf. On 1st October, 107 tons went to Avon Wharf and 181 to Willsbridge.

The last entry in the K&ACC Wharfage Book was 30th January, 1904 when 66 tons 5 cwt. 1 qr. of coal was sent from Tramway Junction to Willsbridge coal wharf for a toll of 5s. 6d. The previous entry had been 22nd January when 87 tons 6½ cwt.had gone from California Colliery to Avon Wharf for a toll of 14s. 6d. No coal had been carried during November 1903 and only 32 tons in December traffic in October was 1,164 tons.

An immense inundation of water had caused California pit to be closed in March 1904 and the colliery plant was sold on 16th February, 1905. On 9th July, 1906 the GWR Traffic Committee was informed by the general manager that 'all traffic on the Avon Tramway has now ceased'.

The A&GR was inspected by Charles Kislingbury, the GWR's Bristol divisional superintendent, on 3rd July, 1913. He found that in places, rails had been taken up to repair fences and that no part of the line had been used for nine years, while north of Oldland Common it had not been utilised for 34 years. In 1912 the tenancies of A&GR banks and wayleaves produced an income of £27, which exactly equalled the expense of the line's maintenance. F.C. Sadler, a mining engineer, revealed that he had an option of 1,000 acres of minerals near the tramway and desired the site of the line at North Common and Warmley. Kislingbury said it would be costly to raise the tramway to railway standards, but that the line had possibilities as existing through running powers could be exercised from Standish Junction to Mangotsfield North Junction, the site of the tramway used as far as the Avon and an extension built across the river to join the GWR's Bristol to Bath line at Keynsham. This interesting proposal proved abortive.

In more recent times the flooded California pit was bought by the West Gloucestershire Water Company and the tramway site from Cherry Garden Lane to Willsbridge sold to them by the GWR in 1935 and used for laying a water main, which ran down the incline, through Willsbridge tunnel and into a valve chamber by the weigh house, Willsbridge.

During the depression in the mid-1920s, coal was mined in the cutting north of Westoncourt Farm, North Common and tubs ran along a small length of tramway. However, the foundations of a house were weakened and mining stopped.

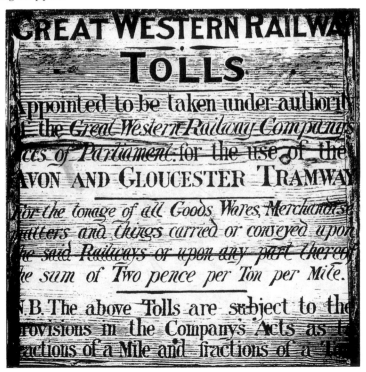

A&GR overbridge, Norman Road, Warmley, 16th February, 1967. *Author*

A&GR rail, chair and key. *Author*

An A&GR rail and stone sleeper block are used to form part of a stile at Hope Cotts, Siston Common, 11th May, 1967. *Author*

Chapter Fourteen

A&GR Permanent Way, Wagons, Locomotives and Tolls

PERMANENT WAY

Edge rails of Birkinshaw's patent design of 1820 were used on the A&GR. They were not quite 'T' section, as there was a groove on one side for an iron key to hold them in the chairs. The minutes say that at least on the Soundwell branch the rails were wrought iron, but the rest were malleable cast iron. The rails were fish-bellied with five webs to each 15 ft rail length. Each rail weighed 28–30 lb./yd, and was 4 in. deep and 2 in. across the tread. The rails for the Soundwell branch were ordered from Foster, Rastrick at £10 ton. In February 1832, the rails, chairs and materials for the siding at Hole Lane coal works cost £80 7s. 5d. In November 1833, J. Bradley was paid £134 7s. 5d. for rails and chairs for the Londonderry branch.

The A&GR chairs weighed 8 lb. each, and measured 7¾ in. by 3¾ in. At joints, two rails were in one chair. Many of the limestone sleeper blocks measured 18 in. by 18 in. and were 10–12 in. deep, but some were 20 in. square. They were set in hard core at intervals of 3 ft 1⅛ in. and wooden plugs, about 5–6 in. deep, were used to drive iron pins into, to fix the chairs to the sleepers. About 25,000 sleepers were needed. As the A&GR quarry at the Backs could supply more than enough for their own needs, Blackwell sold some to the Bristol & Gloucestershire in April 1831. The price of the blocks as they came out of the quarry without boring, was 1s. for a 16 in. square block and 1s. 8d. for a 20 in. square block, delivered at the junction. The A&GR used stone filling between the rails, though Eastwick was asked to use coal ashes rather than gravel as much as possible.

Most of the track was removed for salvage during the 1914–18 war, though lengths of fishbelly rail were used locally in fences and also can be found in various places along the Kennet & Avon Canal. Flat bottom rail weighing 42 lb./yd was used on the branch to California colliery and latterly some steel 40–50 lb./yd. rails at Willsbridge wharf.

WAGONS

On 27th October, 1830 the Western sub-committee inspected and approved a 'pattern wagon' which held 4 tons. The following month it was agreed that 24 be bought and hired to people to use on the line. The Hole Lane pit wished to hire six wagons to 'ascertain their fitness for work', and these were sent to Hole Lane on 30th December. Hoping they could collect coal from collieries not yet connected to the line, Eastwick consulted with Blackwell on whether the wheels of the railway wagons could run for ½ mile on roads without being damaged. Woodward, the contractor for the Bristol & Gloucestershire said that he used his railway wagons on roads for a whole mile without injury. As far as is known, no more came of this interesting suggestion.

In May 1831, it was announced that each wagon cost £26 16s. 11d. and was to be sold to users for £27, but a month later, Eastwick confessed that he had forgotten the cost of the wheels from Stourbridge, which increased the cost to £27 10s. 2d. and it was decided to sell the wagons for £27 10s. By

August 1832 the 24 coal wagons were in use and several more 'can be speedily prepared for paving-stones or other materials'.

In December 1833, the A&GR agreed to reduce the cost of hire of wagons to the Coalpit Heath Company to 5d. ton, on condition that they allowed a drawback of 1s. a ton on coals carried to Reading. All the wagons were in use and the Coalpit Heath Company ordered wheels so they could build some more wagons.

In May 1835 some wagons were sold to the Bristol & Gloucestershire for £829. Between 1836 and 1843, wagons were hired to Hewitt, the Coalpit Heath Company's agent, for £20 per annum.

In 1832 a barge 86 ft long and 16 ft beam was built. It held two tiers of boxes, each box holding 3 tons of coal. Thirty boxes were in each tier. The barge, calculated to make three trips a week, was hired to the Coalpit Heath colliery (together with carts for delivering the coal from this barge at Bath) for £320 per annum. The boxes were carried on flat railway wagons and eased transhipment. In April 1834, Hewitt asked if the railway could dispose of some double box railway wagons and also the boxes. They were sold in April 1835 for:

	£
19 long carriages for coal boxes at £13	247
120 coal boxes at £3 10s.	420
81 trucks for coal boxes at £2	162
	£829

The Act stated that wagons had to have 2 in. high letters giving the name of the owner, the number of the wagon and its weight. Owners were to be responsible for damage done by their wagons. Unlike the Bristol & Gloucestershire Act, it stated that loads must not overhang the sides of the wagons.

At the turn of the century, the California wagons were painted dove grey and were unlettered. They had four-wheel brakes; a sprag was applied to the brake handle and pressed. Californian colliery owned twenty 4-ton tipping coal wagons with sloping ends, three 4-ton coal wagons and one 2-ton coal wagon. The 4-ton wagons were 9 ft long and had 30 in. diameter wheels.

The horse walked between the rails, the driver walking beside the wagon and operating the brakes. The horses were mostly unattended as they knew what to do. Latterly, Major Ollis, of Folly Farm, Bitton, had the contract for supplying the horses, and these were kept in the stable at Londonderry wharf. About two horses were used. On at least one occasion, on a down gradient, the driver failed to apply the sprag to the lever quickly enough and the wagon over-ran the horse and killed it.

At one period, loaded wagons descended the A&GR by gravity and were only drawn back by horses. An elderly man, Mr Ham who had lived at Willsbridge for 60 years, writing in the Bath Weekly Chronicle of 9th June, 1934 said that the wagons, or drams, ran in pairs, a driver on each wagon controlling the speed by handbrake while a young lad accompanied him to open and close the gates of the many level crossings. On reaching the Avon, the trucks automatically tipped and discharged their coal into a waiting barge. When a sufficient number of empty wagons had been collected, horses or donkeys hauled them back to the pithead.

Mr Ham continued:

> I can well remember in my early teens, watching the men and drams emerging from the tunnel and rattling and bumping their way to the boats. On one occasion there was great excitement when the brakes of a truck failed to hold. It rushed out of the tunnel at a terrific speed, smashed clean through the two level crossing gates at Willsbridge, and careered madly towards the river, into which it finally deposited itself with a mighty splash. With the coming of the Midland Railway, the line became obsolete and some 50 years ago I watched the last load go down.

LOCOMOTIVES

It seems unlikely that any locomotives were used on the A&GR, though the Act allowed their use, and the Bristol & Gloucester Act of 1839 said that the Bristol & Gloucester should ensure that on the section used by the A&GR, there were 'sufficient turnouts for all Engines and Carriages used in the conveyance of Coal and articles'.

A&GR TOLLS

The Bristol & Gloucestershire Act stipulated that the toll for Bristol & Gloucestershire traffic going to the A&GR should not exceed 5d. ton/mile and the A&GR fixed the rate for tonnage on its line a toll not exceeding 2d. per ton/mile.

Charges on coal taken from Coalpit Heath and shipped at Avon wharf were:

	s.	d.
Tonnage of Bristol company		5
Tonnage of A&GR		10
Hauling 8d.	1	4
Hire of wagons 8d.		
Shifting and shipping 2½d.		2½
Allowance on every ton,		
1 cwt. or 5% on amount of bill		3
	3	0½

The toll was 2d. ton/mile on the A&GR and the toll board once displayed on the weigh house at Londonderry is now exhibited in Swindon Railway Museum. The wharfage rates were 2d. ton; cranages rates: 2 tons 6d., 3 tons 1s.; 4 tons 1s. 6d. In August 1892, 18 tons of coal were charged 1s. 6d., i.e. 1d. ton ½ mile for the toll from Tramway Junction at the foot of California incline to Willsbridge Coal wharf.

The A&GR accounts were transferred from Bath to Paddington in 1864.

Income from tonnage was £1,086 from August 1832 to June 1833, rose to £2,819 from June 1833 to February 1835, and then declined, being £830 in 1838, £407 in 1844, £245 in 1854, and £83 in 1866–67.

The cutting approaching the north portal of Willsbridge Tunnel, c.1900.
Bristol Museum

The south portal of Willsbridge Tunnel seen on 29th October, 1966.   *Author*

Chapter Fifteen

Description of the A&GR

The Backs, or Avon wharf, as it was more recently called, was opposite Keynsham. The line came to the bank at right angles to the river, with a turntable giving access to a line parallel with the river. It was a short, stone-built wharf with iron ties set in lead between the stones, the stonework being about a yard thick. The wharf was about 15 yds long. Coal was ferried across to the Keynsham side of the river in a flat-bottomed boat attached to a cable.

A stone-built and slate-roof weigh house which held a Foster, Rastrick weighing machine, can still be seen between the wharf and the solidly-built Avonside House, headquarters of the railway and usual meeting place for the Kennet & Avon Western sub-committee when dealing with A&GR affairs. A loop was built by the weigh house so that returning wagons need not pass over the weighbridge. Nearby were the stables, and carpenters' and black-smiths' workshops. A 400 yds-long siding, the site of which is now followed by a cart track, led from Avonside House to the place where stone sleepers were quarried.

Beyond Avonside House, the railway entered a cutting, now well-wooded. It illustrates very well the early method of making a cutting. A plough was used to loosen the soil in the bottom of the cutting, or gunpowder blew up the large stones. Then a horse pulled a scraper like a wheel-less wheelbarrow full of soil to the top of the cutting where it was tipped out on either side into adjoining fields, making a long mound, 20 to 25 yds wide which can still be seen. The sides of the cutting were quite steep in places and were held back by dry stone pitching. Part of the cutting is now filled with water, especially by the occupation overbridge near Londonderry Farm, making it look like a derelict canal. The overbridges on the line mostly had an arch about 9 ft wide, 7 ft high to the springing of the arch and 10 ft to the crown. Beyond this bridge, the cutting has now been filled in and also the overbridge which carries the A4175 obliquely across the line making a 65 ft-long 'tunnel' which is now blocked at one end.

The line comes out on an embankment and the branch from Londonderry rises to meet it. Earthworks and stone sleepers show the course of both lines. There was a passing loop here, which like most of them, branched out on the down side, giving a straight run to trains going against the gradient. This loop was 250 ft long, but most of the others were 200 ft in length. Just before the Bath to Bristol turnpike road was reached was the weighbridge house at Willsbridge wharf, which in recent years has had its roof made flat. The weigh house is in the same style as California colliery and was built by them. This 300 ft wharf siding was opened c.1881, and quite a lot of coal was taken from there by road. An original siding was put in in 1831 for the Bristol Turnpike Trust. The Bath road was crossed on the level – the road had stone setts and there were no level crossing gates.

On the far side the railway entered a cutting where a passing loop was situated, and entered a 156 yds-long tunnel, 8 ft 6 in. high in the centre and its width at track level, 9 ft 5 in. to 10 ft. When it was being bored, £7 18s. 0d. was paid for gunpowder in June 1830 and £4 10s. 0d. for candles. The tunnel was not on the original plan, which made the railway skirt the hill,

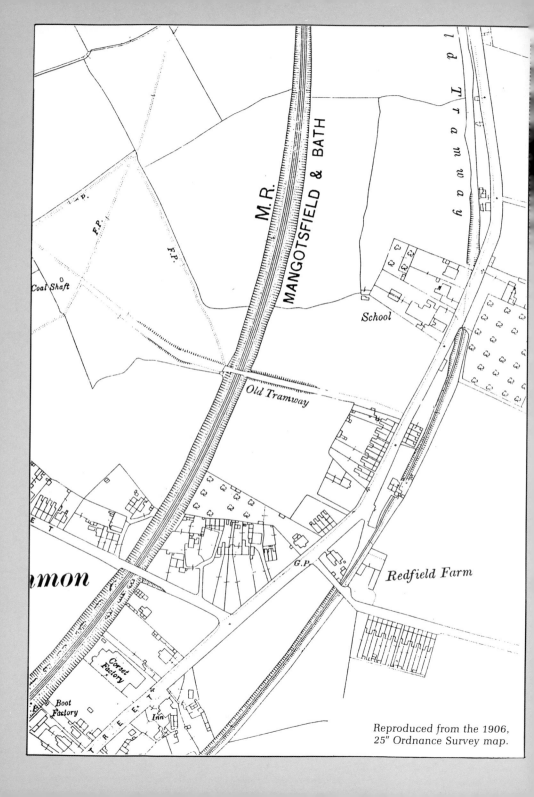

Reproduced from the 1906, 25" Ordnance Survey map.

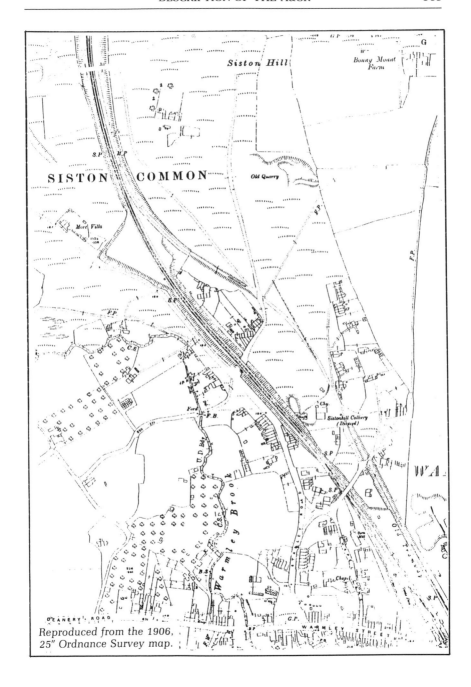

Reproduced from the 1906,
25" Ordnance Survey map.

but was made to hide the railway from the view of a local landowner. During the last war, Bristolians used the tunnel as an air raid shelter for 500 people. The two original ventilation shafts were covered so that light from them could not be seen by enemy planes. (Oddly enough one shaft was round and one square in section.) Bunks were fitted and it was manned voluntarily every night from about 1941–45; a buffet sold coffee, tea, cocoa and sandwiches. After the war, mushrooms were grown there. The tunnel is stone lined; a bend at the north end prevents light from shining through from one end to the other.

At the west portal of the tunnel is an impressive rock cutting about 50 ft deep, cut vertically. It gradually becomes shallower and the line runs on a shelf of a steep hillside. Before the incline to California colliery was a passing loop. The junction of the colliery line with the A&GR was called Tramway Junction. It was a trailing junction, which was a wise choice as runaways down the incline would come to a stop themselves going uphill, and not run out of control down to the level crossing and the river wharves and do damage.

A steep bank rose on the east side and on the west was an impressive vertical wall, 30–40 ft high and still in superb condition. The upward gradient of 1 in 76 was noticeable here. Still with the wall on the west side, there was an embankment on the east as the railway left the hillside and was above the valley floor. The railway passed under Cherry Garden Lane, through what appeared to be a bridge, but was really a 30 ft-long tunnel. The southern half of the tunnel is now lined and supported by Barlow rail across the portal, with fishbelly rails set at right angles across the Barlow rail. The northern half of the tunnel is still unlined, but in 1968, tipping completely blocked it. The 70–80 ft deep cutting north of this tunnel has been filled with rubbish, but until a few years ago was a beautiful wooded glen.

The A&GR passed through a tunnel 73 yds long, which the Midland Railway strengthened with a brick lining for about 30 yds when it built its branch to Bath over the tunnel; the MR milepost 128 was almost exactly above. It is said that as the floor of the tunnel was solid rock, there was no need for stone sleepers and holes were drilled in the floor and the chairs fixed directly to it. At the far end, the A&GR came out into a cutting and crossed under Barry Road and ran parallel to Oldland Common High Street.

After passing under Redfield Lane, a siding led westwards to Hole Lane colliery and further west to Bull Hall colliery. The latter was disused by 1881. In 1851 Hole Lane pit applied for leave to carry water along the A&GR to the brook at Oldland. Permission was granted for a guinea a year. Just north of Redfield Farm, the railway passed under a house in a lined tunnel. A few yards beyond, the A&GR passed diagonally under the A4175 in a 66 yds-long tunnel. This has now been filled in.

The line crossed Victoria Road on the level and curved gently west on an embankment about 4½ ft high. More stone sleepers are visible here. Then followed a shallow, but wide cutting where a passing loop was built. The cutting continued beyond the level crossing over Poplar Road. The line was then on an embankment which rapidly became high as the valley was crossed. A stream was carried under the embankment in a 3 ft high culvert

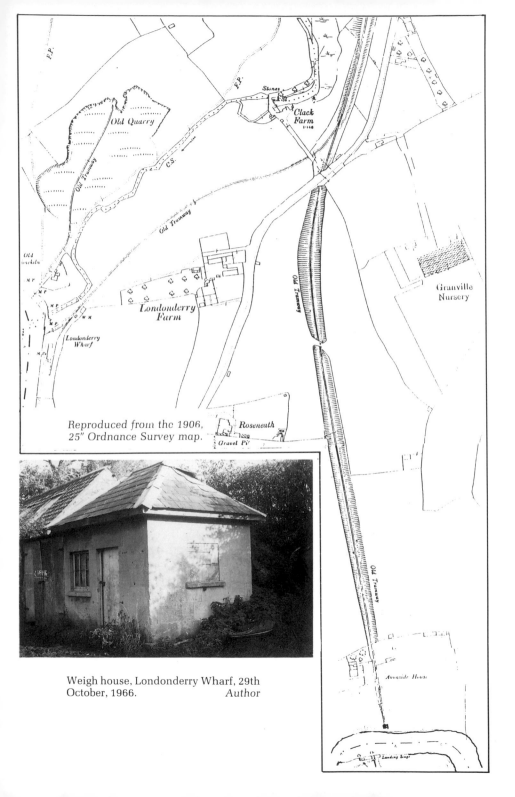

Reproduced from the 1906, 25″ Ordnance Survey map.

Weigh house, Londonderry Wharf, 29th October, 1966.   *Author*

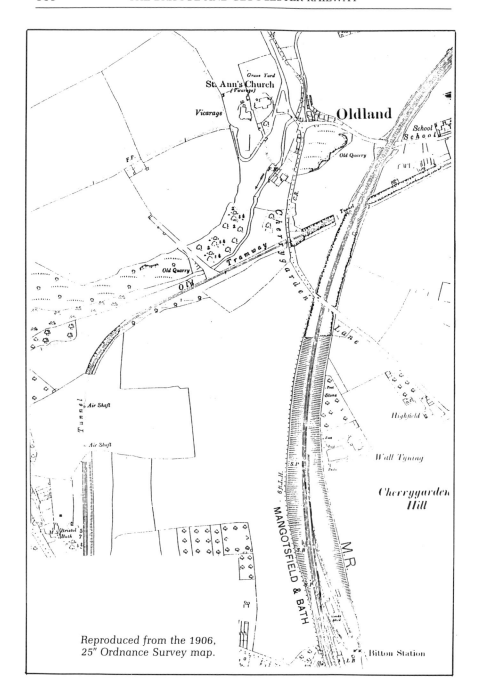

Reproduced from the 1906,
25" Ordnance Survey map.

with drystone lining. After passing a large sandstone quarry, the line went under a high stone bridge carrying a lane immediately west of Warmley Church. The deep cutting became shallow south of the MR station at Warmley and a line diverged east to Goldney pit, with Crown Pit served by another branch on the opposite side of High Street. After entering a cutting, the A&GR passed under a stone overbridge of interesting construction with stringer course and curved wing walls like a canal bridge.

The 1902 25 in. Ordnance Survey plan reveals that about 200 ft of track had been lifted since the 1882 edition and the track bed used for access to houses. Beyond was Siston Common and a passing loop and siding to a clay pit and brickyard which was a source of the line's traffic. Two sidings served Siston Hill colliery. The line across the common was unfenced, most of the remainder being hedged. The cost of fencing, including laying ballast between the rails was £2,060 15s. 3d. The line curved round Siston Hill to avoid making a cutting and was on a 15 ft high embankment. Stone sleepers reveal that the railway was curiously offset to the west side of the embankment. The branch from Soundwell Lower Pit could be seen rising – one of the few places where the load had to be drawn uphill. It joined the main line on the embankment just by the level crossing above Willow Tree Farm. Soundwell Pit was closed in 1853.

When the Midland Railway's Bath branch was built, the A&GR was diverted to avoid crossing the branch twice on the level, as there was insufficient headroom to allow a bridge without seriously interfering with the gradients. This section of the A&GR was avoided by building a new and more direct line beside and on the east side of the MR line. As the Bath branch was not completed until 1869, it is arguable that the A&GR was still expecting traffic at that time, although the last entry in the account book was January 1867.

By the Midland Railway's Mangotsfield South Junction, was a stone overbridge, but the lane it carried was blocked when the MR branch was built. Further on was a skew bridge about 30 yds wide under the Mangotsfield to Goose Green road. About 200 yds north of this bridge was another loop, still marked by stone sleepers. The A&GR terminated by the present Mangotsfield North Junction and in Bristol & Gloucester days, made a trailing junction with it.

The course of the line may still be traced today. Some of the bridges and tunnels are to be seen as well as the wharves and weighbridge houses and quite a number of stone sleeper blocks are still in place.

BRANCHES

Londonderry Wharf was known locally as 'Jacky White's'. The wharf was situated just to the east of the confluence of Warmley Brook with the Avon. The wharf frontage extended for about 90 ft. It was edged with Bath stone held together by iron ties set in lead. The wharf had a slight curve in the centre. Rings were set on the wall for mooring craft. Two sidings led to the wharf while a third served the coal stores. The weigh house was similar in style, though smaller than the one at Avon wharf. From the wharf to the occupation crossing by Clack Farm, there were practically no earthworks

Riverside House, Avon Wharf, the home of the A&GR manager; 29th October, 1966.
Author

Weigh house, Avon Wharf, 29th October, 1966.   *Author*

and the course is now hard to trace, as the shallow cutting by Londonderry Farm has been filled in to level the field, but earthworks where the branch rose to join the Avon wharf line near Willsbridge are clear.

California Colliery. A new 640 yds deep shaft was sunk at California Pit by Abraham Fussell in 1876. The colliery had plant capable of an output of 50 tons of brickettes a day. The coal was very suitable for making brickettes and these formed an important part of the colliery business. The 300 miners raised a maximum weekly tonnage of 1,600–1,700 tons. The branch led from the colliery 450 yds across fields to the edge of the valley above Warmley Brook. An inclined plane on a gradient of about 1 in 10 led down to the A&GR on the other side of the brook. At the head of the plane was a winding house with a galvanised iron roof 20 ft by 10 ft. Inside were two pairs of 6 ft diameter drums on a 14 ft shaft; the winding rope was ⅞ in. in diameter; the incline was self-acting and 150 yds in length. It was in a rock cutting at the top, but lower down was carried across Warmley Brook by a high bridge with a small arch. It seems rather odd that a colliery which had the latest pumping equipment relied on horse, rather than steam power, to take its coal away. In March 1904, Fussell's three collieries at California, Cowhorn Hill and Cadbury Heath were voluntarily wound up.

Londonderry Wharf, looking upstream, 22nd August, 1968.   *Author*

Appendix One

Opening and Closing Dates of Stations

	Opening Passenger	Opening Goods	Closing Passenger	Closing Goods
Fishponds	3.1866	1879	7. 3.1966	13.12.1965
Staple Hill	1.11.1888	–	7. 3.1966	–
Mangotsfield (North Junc. site)	1. 5.1845	1. 5.1845	4. 8.1869	10. 6.1963
Mangotsfield (Station Junc. site)	4. 8.1869	–	7. 3.1966	–
Yate	8. 7.1844	2. 9.1844	4. 1.1965	20. 6.1966
Yate (new station)	15. 5.1989	–	–	–
Wickwar	8. 7.1844	2. 9.1844	4. 1.1965	10. 6.1963
Charfield	8. 7.1844	2. 9.1844	4. 1.1965	6. 9.1965
Berkeley Road	8. 7.1844	2. 9.1844	4. 1.1965	1.11.1966
Coaley	18. 9.1856	25. 8.1856	4. 1.1965	1.11.1966
Frocester	8. 7.1844	2. 9.1844	11.12.1961	11.12.1961
Stonehouse	8. 7.1844	2. 9.1844	4. 1.1965	3. 1.1966
Haresfield	29. 5.1854	–	4. 1.1965	–
Gloucester (new MR station)	12. 4.1896	2. 9.1844	1.12.1975	1. 8.1967

Appendix Two

Industrial Branch Lines & Sidings
Bristol–Gloucester

Down side: Peckett & Sons locomotive works established 1864. East Bristol Collieries Ltd locomotive shunted branch until Kingswood Colliery closed April 1936, after which Peckett used their 0–6–0ST *Nancy*. Branch closed June 1958.

Speedwell	0–4–0ST	Fox, Walker Works No. 281
May	0–6–0ST	Fox, Walker Works No. 286
	0–4–0ST	Peckett Works No. 520
Nancy	0–6–0ST	Peckett Works No. 1067

Up side: before Mangotsfield Station. Mangotsfield Pennant Stone Co. Ltd's siding 1877–1899.

Down side: North of Mangotsfield, Cattybrook Brick Co. Ltd. Works closed 1959. North of brickworks was Shortwood & Parkfield Colliery siding, opened by 1896, taken out of use 26th May, 1940.

Up side: Coalpit Heath Colliery served by mile long LMS branch (formerly the Bristol & Gloucestershire) from Westerleigh. Also spur to GWR. Colliery closed 1950, but line retained for wagon storage until March 1956.

Locomotives:

	0–4–0T	Fletcher, Jennings Works No. 58
	0–6–0ST	Fox, Walker Works No. 326
Lord Roberts	0–6–0ST	Peckett Works No. 825
Lord Salisbury	0–6–0ST	Peckett Works No. 1041
	4wDM	Ruston & Hornsby Works No. 242869

Up side: Yate No. 1 (near Milepost 119) opened pre-1854 and closed *c*.1888 and Yate No. 2 (118 miles 54 chains) 1896–1906.

Up side: Old Wood Colliery, Rangeworthy, 118¼ miles 1883–1885.

Down side: Wickwar, siding to cider works, 1860–1954.

Up side: Slimbridge Storage Depot, operated in conjunction with Quedgeley munitions factory. Line built by Messrs Pauling & Co. Ltd work starting about November 1915. From 106.53 miles near Tumpy Green, to a wharf on the Gloucester & Berkeley Ship Canal at Patch Bridge. Sidings served extensive complex of ammunition storage sheds. Locomotives stabled in shed near Oldhurst Farm.

Locomotives (shared with the Quedgeley Factory and allocation to which site is unknown):

Newcastle	0–6–0ST	Manning, Wardle Works No. 1532
	0–6–0ST	Manning, Wardle Works No. 1928
Cefn	0–6–0ST	Hunslet Works No. 256
Quedgeley	0–4–0T	LSWR 'S14' class No.147
	0–6–0ST	Manning, Wardle Works No. 1561
	0–6–0ST	Hudswell, Clarke, Works No. 494

Up side: Branch from immediately north of Frocester station to sand and gravel pits at Frampton on Severn about 3½ miles distant, to supply building materials for construction of National Shipyards at Beachley, Chepstow and Portbury. Mile long branch line from workings to wharf on the Gloucester & Berkeley Ship Canal at Splatt Bridge. Junction at Frocester brought into use 20th May, 1918 and removed 27th April, 1924.

Locomotives:

Inveresk No. 1	0–4–0ST	Hawthorn, Leslie Works No. 2344
Phoenix	0–6–0ST	Manning, Wardle Works No. 1449
Gibbon	0–6–0ST	Hunslet Works No. 545

Up side: Stonehouse, Hoffman Gloucester Ltd siding 6th February, 1940–18th November, 1966.

Locomotive:

4wDM	Muir Hill Works No. 29

Down side: Stonehouse Coal Concentration Depot 7th October, 1966–1989.

Locomotive:

Dougal	0–4–0DM	Drewry 2251/Vulcan Foundry Works No. D77

Dow Mac (Concrete) Ltd, Naas Lane, Quedgeley, Up side, served by sidings leading from BR/MOD exchange sidings.

Locomotive

0–4–0DE	Ruston & Hornsby Works No. 418602

Up side: National Filling Factory No. 5, Quedgeley, 96.45 miles. Factory construction started October 1915 and came into production March 1916. Trains of workers ran from Cheltenham, Stroud and Gloucester into passenger platform in factory premises. Factory closed post-1921 and track lifted by December 1925.

Locomotives:

(See entry for Slimbridge Storage Depot.)

In 1938, the site of the Quedgeley Filling Factory was used for an RAF Maintenance & Storage Depot. Rail traffic ceased August 1976.

Locomotives:

No. 150	0–4–0DM	John Fowler Works No. 22498
No. 153	0–4–0DM	John Fowler Works No. 22603
No. 154	0–4–0DM	John Fowler Works No. 22604
No. 157	0–4–0DM	Robert Stephenson & Hawthorn Works No. 6979
No. 167	0–4–0DM	John Fowler Works No. 22876
No. 168	0–4–0DM	John Fowler Works No. 22877
No. 213	0–4–0DM	John Fowler Works No. 22960
No. 221	0–4–0DM	John Fowler Works No. 22968
No. 236	4wDM	Ruston & Hornsby Works No. 210477
No. 237	4wDM	Ruston & Hornsby Works No. 210478
No. 241	0–4–0DM	John Fowler Works No. 22995
	4wDM	Rolls Royce Works No. 10242
	4wDM	Rolls Royce Works No. 10244
Army 243	0–4–0DM	John Fowler Works No. 22890
Army 244	0–4–0DM	John Fowler Works No. 22971

Sidings to Gloucester Gas Works opened after 1920 and closed 1970.

Locomotives:

	4wPM	
No. 2	4wDM	F.C. Hibberd Works No. 2639
	0–4–0DM	John Fowler Works No. 4000014
	4wDM	Ruston & Hornsby Works No. 321731

Gloucester Railway Carriage & Wagon Co. established 1860. Shunting in works yard by locomotives until 1961 and then by dumper trucks.

Locomotives:

Tiger	0–4–0ST	Manning, Wardle (?)
Siam	0–4–0ST	Sharp, Stewart Works No. 2472
Henry Wright	0–4–0ST	Manning, Wardle Works No. 1501
Fox	0–4–0ST	Avonside Works No. 913 (ex-GWR No. 1391)
Aberdare	0–6–0ST	Avonside Works No. 1411
Phoenix	0–4–0ST	Andre Barclay Works No. 1285
Badgeworth Hall	0–4–0	(Fireless steam locomotive) W.G. Bagnall Works No. 2871

Appendix Three

Locomotive Allocations 31st December, 1947

Bristol 22A

Class '3P' 2–6–2T
119, 174

Class '2P' 4–4–0
423

Class '3P' 4–4–0
741

Class '4P' Compound 4–4–0
935, 1028, 1030

Class '1P' 0–4–4T
1389, 1411

Class '1F' 0–6–0T
1706, 1874

Class '2F' 0–6–0
3094

Class '3F' 0–6–0
3178, 3204, 3228, 3419, 3436, 3439, 3444, 3464, 3593, 3712, 3734

Class '4F' 0 -6–0
3853, 3928, 3953, 4112, 4135, 4169, 4266, 4411, 4424, 4466, 4534, 4536, 4537, 4569

Class '5P5F' 4–6–0
4804, 4812, 4843, 4855, 5272

Class '5XP' 'Jubilee' 4–6–0

5561	Saskatchewan	5682	Trafalgar
5570	New Zealand	5685	Barfleur
5572	Eire	5690	Leander
5662	Kempenfelt	5694	Bellerophon
5663	Jervis		

Ex- SDJR 'Sentinel' 0–4–0T
7190

Class '3F' 0–6–0T
7544, 7550, 7678

Ex-LYR '0F' 0–4–0ST
11212

Total: 56

Gloucester 22B

Class '2P' 4–4–0
437, 523, 530

Class '4P' Compound 4–4–0
1001, 1019, 1025, 1027, 1039, 1058, 1074, 1097

Class '1P' 0–4–4T
1251, 1303, 1353, 1365

Class '0F' 0–4–0T
1530, 1537

Class '1F' 0–6–0T
1720, 1727, 1870

Class '5F' 2–6–0
2922

Class '2F' 0–6–0
3062

Class '3F' 0–6–0
3213, 3257, 3258, 3263, 3344, 3373, 3427, 3506, 3507, 3604, 3645, 3754, 3791

Class '4F' 0–6–0
3846, 3887, 3924, 3932, 3978, 4045, 4167, 4175, 4229, 4235, 4269, 4272, 4553, 4576, 4585

Class '3F' 0–6–0T
7237, 7619, 7620, 7635

Total: 54

Gloucester station with No. 437 waiting to leave on 1st September, 1926.

H.C. Casserley

Appendix Four

Observations at the south portal of Wickwar Tunnel, Saturday 12th August, 1961

No. of Engine	Time pm	
45626	2.25	Up express, 10 coaches
73046	2.30	Down express, 10 coaches
D21	2.40	Down 'Devonian', about 10 coaches
4914	2.45	Up express, 10 coaches
73031	2.54	Up express, 10 coaches
92136	3.05	Down 'Pines Express', 12 coaches
44920	3.07	Up express, 10 SR coaches
6831	3.13	Up express, 10 coaches
45324	3.20	Up express, 9 coaches
4087	3.26	Up express, 11 coaches
44742	3.32	Up express, 8 coaches
6904	3.38	Up express, 11 coaches
73155	3.42	Down express, 11 coaches
46137	3.47	Down express, 11 coaches
45575	3.50	Up express, 14 coaches
92131	3.58	Up express, 8 coaches
45660	4.01	Down express, 10 coaches
44918	4.02	Up express, 10 coaches
7904	4.10	Up express, 13 coaches
92139	4.18	Up express, 8 coaches
6931	4.24	Up express, 10 coaches
44839	4.34	Up express, 10 coaches
5992	4.40	Up express, 9 coaches
6981	4.41	Down light engine
4904	4.51	Up express, 10 coaches
73138	5.02	Down stopping, 3 coaches
5024	5.03	Up express, 9 coaches
92138	5.14	Up express, 9 coaches
48351	5.22	Up freight, 50 wagons
5058	5.28	Up express, 10 coaches
92128	5.43	Down express, 5 coaches

BR Standard class '5' No. 73138 from Derby shed, passes below a combined aqueduct and footbridge south of Wickwar Tunnel with the 2.40 pm Worcester–Bristol, on 12th August, 1961. *Author*

Bristol shed on 27th May, 1935 with Nos. 1030, 3173 and 1228 simmering in the
sunlight.   *H.C. Casserley*

No. 41748 with the 9.55 train from Dursley seen here at Coaley Junction station on 9th
March, 1956 (the coach is No. 20509).   *R.M. Casserley*

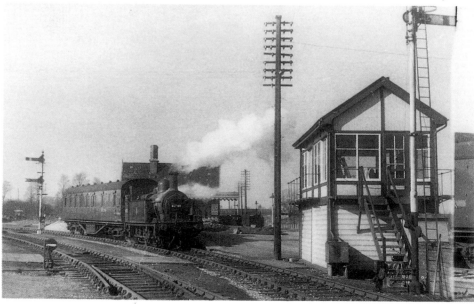

Appendix Five

Logs of Runs

(A) GLOUCESTER TO BRISTOL *(in minutes and seconds)*

Distance	Locomotive	45662	45682	W51092/W51064	D120	D20	D1677	D112
	No. of coaches	11	9	3 car dmu	10	11	7	12
	Date	16. 8.56	24. 8.60	9.10.65	5. 9.63	15. 6.63	1.10.66	18. 7.69
—	Gloucester							
32	Mangotsfield	38	36	47	46	39	45	48
37	Bristol T.M.	25	19	53	42	20	18	00[a]

(B) LOGS OF RUNS BRISTOL TO GLOUCESTER *(in minutes and seconds)*

Distance	Locomotive	44809	45509	44917	73003	D146	D152	D138	D144	D41	D42	D95
	No. of coaches	9	9	4	9	11	11	9	10	11	8	9
	Date	3. 3.55	15. 3.55	16. 8.56	10. 8.60	18. 4.63	15. 6.63	27. 8.63	10. 4.64	20. 5.64	9.10.65	2. 8.69
—	Bristol T.M.											
5	Mangotsfield	13	13	36	36	35	34	34	37	34	39	40
37	Gloucester	44	58	25[c]	44[b]	47[b,d]	34	25[b,d]	30[b,d]	34[b,d]	54	20

Notes:

- a = *via Filton*
- b = *from Mangotsfield only*
- c = *from Mangotsfield North Junction only*
- d = *stopped at Berkeley Road*

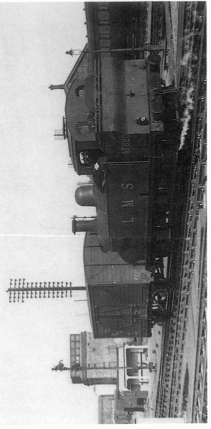

0–6–0, No. 47620 seen here at Gloucester on 8th September, 1945.   *R.M. Casserley*

Staff employed by the B&GR, 1844

Stations	Super-intendents	Carriage Clerks	Goods Clerks	Inspector of Police	Switchmen	Policemen	Carriage Porters	Goods Porters	Passenger Guards	Goods Guards
Bristol	1								5	4
Carriage & Goods			2	1			1	8		
Lawrence Hill					1					
Fishponds					1					
Mangotsfield		1				1				
Yate		1				1				
Carriage							1			
Wickwar		1			1					
Charfield		1				1				
Carriage & Goods							1			
Berkeley Rd		1				1				
Frocester		1				1				
Carriage							1			
Stonehouse		1				1				
Carriage & Goods							1			
Total	1	7	2	1	3	6	5	8	5	4

Salaries and Wages, 1844

Goods clerk:	£100 per annum
Passenger and parcels clerk:	£90 per annum
(Clerks to provide £300 security)	
Guard:	21 shillings per week
Switchman:	18 shillings per week
Policeman and porter:	15 shillings per week
(plus a suit of clothes per annum)	

Quantity of Coal taken down the A&GR from the Bristol & Gloucestershire Railway 1st January–31st December, 1843

Week	ending	Tons	Cwt.	No. of wagons	Week	ending	Tons	Cwt.	No. of wagons
Jan.	6	213	16	48	July	7	209	17	47
	13	201	12	45		14	123	4	28
	20	320	2	72		21	262	18	61
	27	260	17	60		28	193	9	43
Feb.	3	171	1	39	Aug.	4	167	17	38
	10	150	15	34		11	199	9	45
	17	175	8	40		18	207	0	47
	24	191	1	43		25	196	10	44
Mar.	3	288	2	65	Sept.	1	277	12	63
	10	239	1	54		8	193	3	44
	17	159	9	36		15	256	15	59
	24	195	18	44		22	181	16	39
	31	160	5	36		29	262	1	61
Apr.	7	160	4	36	Oct.	6	102	6	23
	14	119	10	27		13	260	0	60
	21	154	8	35		20	185	14	40
	28	163	9	37		27	248	16	57
May	5	264	11	61	Nov.	3	149	0	34
	12	142	14	32		10	97	18	22
	19	200	8	45		17	84	7	20
	26	363	8	82		24	212	13	48
June	2	237	12	54	Dec.	1	224	8	50
	9	81	8	19		8	199	10	45
	16	253	2	58		15	249	18	57
	23	444	18	101		22	250	12	58
	30	254	12	58		29	83	16	20
							10,650	12	2,414

Average per week 204 tons 16 cwt. in 46 wagons.

Bibliography

Locomotive & Train Working in the Nineteenth Century; E.L. Ahrons; Heffer.
Titled Trains of the Western; C.J. Allen; Ian Allan.
Action Station; C. Ashworth; Patrick Stephens.
The Dramway; R. Barber;Avon Industrial Buildings Trust.
The Rise of the Midland Railway 1844–1874; E.G. Barnes; Allen & Unwin.
The Midland Main Line; E.G. Barnes; Allen & Unwin.
British Locomotive Catalogue 1825–1923 Volume 3A; B. Baxter; Moorland.
Locomotives of the LSWR, Vol. 2: The Drummond Classes; D.L. Bradley; Wild Swan Publications.
Regional History of Railways, Vol. 13, Thames & Severn; R.A. Christiansen; David & Charles.
The Kennet & Avon Canal; K.B. Clew; David & Charles.
Closed Passenger & Goods Station; C.R. Clinker; Avon Anglia.
Track Layout Diagrams of the Great Western Railway and BR Western Region, Sections 19, 20, 35; R.A. Cooke (pub. by the compiler).
The Midland Railway, A Chronology; J. Gough; Railway & Canal Historical Society.
Mangotsfield Past; Downend Local History Society.
Mangotsfield Picture Past; Downend Local History Society.
British Railway Accidents of the Twentieth Century; J.A.B. Hamilton; Allen & Unwin.
Trains to Nowhere; J.A.B. Hamilton, Allen & Unwin.
Industrial Locomotives of South Western England; R. Hateley; Industrial Railway Society.
Industrial Locomotives of Central Southern England; R. Hateley; Industrial Railway Society.
LMS Engine Sheds, Vol. 2; C. Hawkins and G. Reeve; Wild Swan Publications.
Midland Railway Carriages; R.E. Lacy and G. Dow; Wild Swan Publications.
The Birmingham & Gloucester Railway; P.J. Long and W.V. Awdry; Alan Sutton.
History of the Great Western Railway; E.T. Macdermot, revised by C.R. Clinker; Ian Allan.
Historic Railway Disasters; O.S. Nock; Ian Allan.
Bristol Suburban; M. Oakley; Redcliffe.
An Historical Survey of the Midland in Gloucestershire; P. Smith; OPC.
History of the Birmingham & Gloucester, and the Bristol & Gloucester Railways; C. Stretton; Methuen.
Midland Railway; C. Stretton; Methuen.
Red for Danger; L.T.C. Rolt; John Lane, the Bodley Head.
Midland Railway; F.S. Williams; Bemrose.

Minute books: Avon & Gloucestershire Railway; Birmingham & Bristol Railway; Kennet & Avon Canal; Midland Railway.

Newspapers: Aris's *Birmingham Gazette*; *Bath Chronicle*; *Bristol Gazette*; *Bristol Mirror*; Felix Farley's *Bristol Journal*; *Gloucester Journal*; *Railway Times*; *Western Daily Press*.

Magazines: *British Railway Journal*; *Engineering*; *Illustrated London News*; *LMS Magazine*; *Railway Magazine*; *Railway Observer*; *The Engineer*; *Trains Illustrated*.

A clean No. 3181, 0-6-0 standing in Bristol shed on 20th April, 1934 with No. 3181, 3875 in the background. *H.C. Casserley*

Gloucester station in September, 1949 with No. 41001 waiting for the off.

H.C. Casserley

Index

ff – and following pages